DNA of a
Christ Follower

The 8 Essential Traits

Jesus Calling

Eph 3: 14-21

DNA of a Christ Follower

The 8 Essential Traits

Daren Wride

Deep Wild Communications

Library and Archives Canada Cataloging in Publication
Wride, Daren, 1964-
DNA of a Christ Follower / Daren Wride
ISBN 978-0-9783393-1-9
1. Christian Living
2. Christian Ministry and Church Leadership

Unless otherwise noted:
Scriptures are taken from the Holy Bible, Today's New International
Version™ TNIV®, Copyright ©2001, 2005, by International Bible
Society®. All rights reserved worldwide.
Printed in Canada

For related resources and information
on booking the author to speak,
please visit
ChristFollowerDNA.com

To the people of Valleyview Alliance Church

Who illustrated these traits
long before I articulated them

Contents

Section I
The Personal Challenge

Section II
The Traits

Section III
The Church's Challenge

Section I

The Personal Challenge

CHAPTER 1

Introduction

A body on the ground. Flashing lights. Yellow police tape securing the area. A detective wearing latex gloves shining a flashlight, looking closely at the scene. A pause, a hair carefully lifted from the victim's clothing and placed in a bag. It is not the victim's color. Lab work later identifies some key markers in the hair. These markers match a suspect who is eventually convicted of the crime beyond a reasonable doubt.

If you watch any television whatsoever, you've seen many variations of the above scenario. And while it doesn't work quite so quickly and easily in real life as in the crime dramas, DNA analysis has made a huge difference in police work over the last few decades—not to mention medical and anthropological studies.

DNA—deoxyribonucleic acid—the building block of the chromosomes, the genetic code of all organisms (except some viruses), the matter that is responsible for the transmission of hereditary characteristics from parents to children. A piece of your hair, a flake of your skin, your blood, even your saliva can be identified as yours by the presence of your unique DNA fingerprint. DNA matches are useful in identifying criminals, victims of crime, and the propensity for some diseases. Increasingly, DNA technology is being used for medical research and the development of new treatments. In short, DNA is a physical marker, a genetic snapshot of a person or organism.

Is there a similar marker, a nonphysical DNA that demonstrates someone's spiritual make-up?

Several years ago I had the privilege of spending a week at Kananaskis Lodge in the Rocky Mountain foothills near Calgary, Alberta. I was there for a week of training with Sonlife Ministries.

One of my instructors for the week pointed out that if people in our churches come to three hours of church activity per week, we have only the equivalent of six 24-hour days per year to build into their lives. Due to this limited window, we need to be realistic about what we can do in that amount of time. We also need to be focused and deliberate about exactly what we are trying to accomplish. He said, in essence, "You are supposed to be a disciple, and you are called to make disciples. But have you defined what a disciple is? Have you articulated the non-negotiable qualities that you must build into people's lives for them to be successful followers of Jesus Christ?" Those were disturbing questions. Actually, it was my inner answers that were even more disturbing: "No" and "No." His next question bothered me even more: "Are you structuring your teaching, your leading, your church life in such a way as to develop those qualities?"

Those questions began to dominate my mind. I was in my tenth year of pastoring and had tasted at least a small measure of success in ministry. I was becoming entrenched in a way of leading and developing a church, which, while it brought people to faith in Christ and caused some growth, was neither as effective nor as efficient as I felt it could be. It wasn't clear in either my own mind or the minds of those I was leading exactly what it was we were trying to accomplish in people's lives once they identified with Jesus. As a result, my efforts and the ministries of the church lacked focus. There was no mechanism to say "We should do this" or "We shouldn't do that" and no meaningful way to measure outcomes.

And so I was introduced to what my instructor referred to as the DDP—Description of a Discipled Person. BUT, in a stroke of educational genius (or downright nastiness—I waver in my opinion) neither the instructor nor the accompanying Sonlife material gave us such a description. Instead, we were challenged to define, on our own, eight or fewer qualities that were the non-negotiable characteristics of a disciple or follower of Jesus Christ—qualities, which if someone possessed them, would make that person an unmistakable, rock solid disciple of Jesus Christ.

The week continued with more thought-provoking teaching. But I was nagged by the idea that I was called to do something and was in fact attempting to do something—make disciples—without ever having clearly defined the target. And I had been doing so for ten years! At the same time, I knew there were hundreds, perhaps thousands of pastors functioning just as I was, not to mention the millions of Christians who, like me, were unclear on what it meant to be a disciple. I felt like rewinding time and starting pastoral ministry, and a large portion of my Christian life, all over again.

That week began what has been one of the most profitable exercises I have ever done as a Christian leader, and as a follower of Jesus. While it's easy to come up with a list of several dozen qualities a disciple is supposed to have, trying to boil such a list down to eight or fewer is quite painful and difficult, as our instructor predicted.

Why eight or fewer? Why not just make a list of whatever comes up and go with that number? Realistically, eight is probably even too many. Few people have the capacity to focus on more than two or three objectives at once. Phone numbers have seven digits, in addition to the area code, for a reason. I've found that a limit of eight allows most if not all of the possible qualities to be condensed and combined in a logical way, while still giving a number that is not completely overwhelming.

My response to the challenge began with a reading of the New Testament, making a list of every possible character quality I could find. Some were stated outright in the verses, some were implied. I ended up with about 25 typed pages, two columns each, nearly two thousand individual entries. Many qualities were repeated in the list, but there were still dozens of possibilities. I then began to boil them down. I asked for input from other people. I read descriptions of Christ Followers that I came across. In time, I managed to condense my list to eight. I have taught through these traits in several churches and have become increasingly convinced both of the need to articulate such a list, and that the ones I have settled on are indeed some essential character qualities of a Christ Follower. I believe that if people possess and are growing in these characteristics, they will be identifiable as biblical followers of Jesus Christ.

Once when I was planning a series of services around these topics, someone made the comment that it was kind of like the DNA of a Christ Follower, the unique identifiable features of a disciple of Jesus Christ. And so my original "DDP" became the DNA of a Christ Follower.

If you consider yourself a Christ Follower—and forgive me if this comes across as overly dramatic—this idea of identifying some essential accompanying character traits could revolutionize the way you approach your Christian life. You see, too often we get caught up in what a Christian is supposed to do and forget that it's about the heart, about character. What we do flows from who and what we are.

The character qualities described in this book explain who we are, or at least who we are called to be—the genetic markers that will identify us as followers of Jesus Christ. Some of the traits are obvious; they may have already come to your mind. But others are a bit more surprising, and might not be on the list most of us would generate apart from a survey of scripture. The development of these qualities will make you into "a good soldier of Christ Jesus" (2 Timothy 2.3), a person who is both salty salt and unhidden light (Matthew 5), someone who "bears much fruit" (John 15) and who will "be confident and unashamed before him at his coming" (1 John 2.28). Since we reproduce what we are, these traits will ensure that we are disciples who make disciples, not merely cultural Christians who focus on getting people to pray a prayer and then allow them to carry on unchanged, impotent to challenge and transform our culture, participating in the coming of the Kingdom.

If you are in "spiritual exploration mode", still trying to figure out if Jesus Christ is who he said he was— "the way and the truth and the life" (John 14.6) —this study may be helpful for you as well. As you read, you will grow in your understanding of what the Bible says a Christ Follower is, versus the many caricatures you see in the media and sometimes, unfortunately, in the church. I hope this will help you better understand what it is that God will do in you if you respond to His call to receive forgiveness through Jesus.

It is important to state early on that what is primarily being described in these pages is not the way of salvation, the way to connect with your Creator, though this will be discussed briefly. The Bible teaches that we come to God through Jesus Christ, by repentance and faith, both of which are gifts from God.

> *"I have declared to both Jews and Greeks that they*
> *must turn to God in repentance and have faith in our*
> *Lord Jesus Christ." (Acts 20.21)*

Repentance is a mental, emotional, spiritual, moral, total-person U-turn, a change of heart and mind leading to a change of action. It is turning from our way of doing life to God's plan for doing life. It is a turn from our self-sufficiency to a life of dependence on God, a turn from disconnectedness with our Creator to the connectedness and relationship with him for which we've been made.

Faith is not merely a belief that Jesus existed or that he lived and died and rose. When people are told, *"Believe in the Lord Jesus Christ and you will be saved"* (Acts 16.31) it is a call to accept that he died in their place. As it says in 1 Peter, *"He himself bore our sins in His body on the cross, so that we might die to sins and live for righteousness."* (1 Peter 2.24) The way of salvation, the way to connect with God, is to repent and believe. The character qualities defined and expounded upon in this book are the results of that repentance and faith, a thorough expression of the kind of life God both calls us to and creates in us through Jesus.

One obvious question about this book's approach is, "Why not simply use some of the biblical lists like the Fruit of the Holy Spirit (Galatians 5), the Beatitudes (Matthew 5) or some of the other character lists in the New Testament letters?" My answer is that none of those lists were intended to be a comprehensive synthesis of all possible character qualities, though undoubtedly if we lived out either of those lists we would be doing well. This compilation is, in essence, a theme study including all of those lists and going beyond them to identify and isolate qualities that are mentioned or implied throughout the New Testament. Another fair question is, "Why not include the Old Testament?" In fact, while the OT wasn't included in the making of the original list, apart from the ever-present "faith and obedience" we see in most major Old Testament characters, it is very much included in rounding out and explaining the character qualities that were discovered.

On the character level, the ultimate goal of the Christian life is to become like Jesus. In a word, the target is Christlikeness. The role of church leadership is to facilitate the accomplishment of this goal:

> "...to equip his people for works of service, so that the
> body of Christ may be built up until we all reach unity
> in the faith and in the knowledge of the Son of God
> and become mature, attaining to the whole measure of
> the fullness of Christ." (Ephesians 4.12-13)

The traits highlighted in this study should be recognized as character traits of Jesus himself. So, properly understood, the DNA of a Christ Follower is the DNA of Jesus himself, planted in us through the new birth, increasingly being revealed as we move toward maturity.

Once a person repents of their sins and places their faith in Jesus Christ for forgiveness and salvation, they begin the journey towards becoming like Jesus. What will that look like? What character qualities should be nurtured and developed? What does it actually mean to be a follower of Jesus Christ? This book is my current answer to those questions. I have written it to challenge pastors and Christian leaders involved in discipleship to clarify what exactly it is they are trying, with the Spirit's help, to achieve in people's lives. I have also written for the many individuals who use such books for personal devotions and small group fodder. Indeed it is has been forged in and for the practical world of local church ministry because that is the context in which disciples are made.

In the end, your list might look different than mine, but I suspect you will see this as a fairly comprehensive description of a Christ Follower. I hope it will help you, as it has helped me, to shape any ministry you are involved with into a disciple-making effort and, more importantly, to be shaped into a passionate pursuer of Jesus.

———•◆•———

CHAPTER 2

Christ Follower Versus Christian

M y maternal grandfather graduated from Bible school in Min-
nesota in 1928 and became a circuit-riding pastor in the In-
terlake region of Manitoba. He served in that area until he passed
away in the late 70s. As a result, my mother was born into a Christian home. She went away to nursing school and eventually found
herself working in the northern community of Grand Rapids, Manitoba, where there was a major hydroelectric project.

One day a "Mountie" (Royal Canadian Mounted Police officer)
delivered a lady in labor to the hospital and bet my future mom two-
bits (that's 25 cents for you young'uns) that the baby would be a boy.
Thus began a classic northern-Canadian relationship—a nurse and
a Mountie. My mother succeeded in pulling off what is known as
a "flirt and convert" (NOT a recommended evangelism technique)
and, by the grace of God, rather than being drawn away from the
faith by this thoroughly pagan young man, helped bring him to faith.
As a result, like my mother, I was born into a home where both parents were believers. And despite my mother's questionable outreach
technique, I will be eternally grateful that I was born into a family
centered on Christ, the gospel, and the church.

We were quite involved in church life—Sunday morning, Sunday
evening, midweek events of various kinds, occasional evangelistic
crusades—and during the summers of my elementary years I went
to Silver Bay Bible Camp in southern Manitoba, a camp that had
been started by my grandfather in the 1930s.

One night when I was about eight or nine years old my grandfather and uncle, who co-led the camp at the time, shared the story of how Jesus came and lived and died and rose, and how his actions applied, or could apply to me. Even though I'd heard it dozens if not hundreds of times in the past, for some reason this time the lights went on. I understood that Jesus hadn't just died, he'd died for me. I realized that when the Bible says, "For God so loved the world," it included me. It meant that God loved me and gave his Son for me.

At the end of the chapel service they asked anyone who wanted to accept Jesus as Saviour to stay, and I, along with a cousin who was sitting beside me, stayed. We were sitting near the back and, after most of the others had left, we went to the front to do what we needed to do. But my uncle and grandfather, who were already counselling one tearful young man, just looked at us and said, "Get out of here!" We were stunned. We just stood there not knowing what to say. "Get out of here!" they said again and shooed us out of the chapel. It wasn't the reaction I'd expected when going forward to receive Christ as my Saviour. To be fair, they had good reason to believe that we were hanging around just to be disruptive and cause trouble, but in this rare case that wasn't our motivation. We wanted to get saved. I often refer to this event as my "attempted conversion."

My cousin and I left the chapel service confused and teary eyed. For many years I remained afraid of dying and felt like I still needed to do something to receive forgiveness. The popularity of end-times teaching and the arrival of what I refer to as a Christian horror movie series, beginning with A Thief in the Night, only added to my terror.

When I was thirteen or fourteen, reading the Bible through for the first time after signing up at the church to do so in a year, I came across a simple verse of scripture, in which Jesus was speaking following his feeding of the 5000. He said, *"All whom the Father gives me will come to me, and whoever comes to me I will never drive away."* (John 6.37)

His words stopped me cold. I realized at that moment that when I had responded in faith, as best I could way back at that camp, and was chased out of the chapel, Jesus wasn't the one doing the chasing—he never drives away anyone who comes to him. Which means he accepts, receives and embraces those who come to him. The fact that I never got to "pray a prayer" was irrelevant—I was coming to him. I was beginning to follow him.

What's the Difference Between a Christian and a Christ Follower?

At first glance, there doesn't seem to be much difference between a Christian and a Christ Follower: A Christian is assumed to be the same thing as a Christ Follower, and a Christ Follower is of course a Christian. A little research, however, reveals that the current usage and meaning of the term 'Christian' doesn't align with what it means to be a follower of Jesus Christ. There is, in fact, a massive difference between the two.

The word 'Christian' (Greek 'Christianos') shows up sparsely in the New Testament. We read in Acts 11.26, *"The disciples were called Christians first at Antioch."* It is probably safe to say that at this point, there was perfect correspondence between the functional meaning of 'Christian' and 'disciple of Jesus/Christ Follower'. At that time, any Christian was, in fact, a follower of Jesus Christ. However, it seems to be implied by this verse that the label was coined by those outside the faith, possibly as a term of ridicule.

Later, in Acts 26, Paul shares his story and the Gospel with King Agrippa, and Agrippa asks Paul, *"Do you think that in such a short time you can persuade me to be a Christian?"* (Acts 26.28) This indicates that the usage of the word had moved beyond the region of Antioch and had become a popularized term used, at least by those outside the Christian faith, to describe people who identified themselves as followers of Jesus Christ. It also indicates that this new religion was beginning to be seen as distinct from Judaism rather than just being a sect within that larger religion.

The third and final instance of the word is in 1 Peter where disciples are instructed regarding suffering, and told that their suffering should not be for wrong doing. *"However, if you suffer as a Christian, do not be ashamed, but praise God that you bear that name."* (1 Peter 4.16) While it may be that at this point the word is still used primarily by those outside the faith as a charge or attack against those identified with Christ, there is at least a hint here that the word was beginning to be accepted by disciples as a descriptor of themselves as followers of Jesus Christ.

The point is that in the early days of the church, a Christian was a Christ Follower, a disciple of Jesus Christ, a believer in Jesus Christ, a brother or sister of others who did the same.

However, since then, the word Christian has been cheapened by its usage. It's been applied over the years to groups of people who fight against and kill other groups of people, who in some cases are also called Christians. And they have done this not just as citizens of a given country in a given time and place, but in some cases because they are Christians. How is that possible? It makes no sense given what the word used to mean.

Many people around the world think that North America is a Christian continent, and that what they see oozing out through popular culture is Christianity. I recently listened to an international worker (aka missionary) who works in a primarily Islamic country. He shared that Muslims see all of North America as Christian, including high-profile musicians, movie stars, and politicians. All of our celebrities, regardless of their conduct or misconduct, are considered Christian! They see us, in the words of this cross-cultural worker as "shameful rebels," and as individualists who care about no one but ourselves. They don't see us as religious because they observe that we don't pray and that we're shameless and decidedly immodest. He shared how even Muslim men who watch made-in-America pornography believe this porn is a product of Christianity because it comes from North America. Toss in the lack of a discernible gap between the divorce rates, ethical standards, entertainment practices, usage of time, money, and possessions of those who call themselves Christians and those who do not, and it's clear that something has changed, that people who are called or who call themselves Christians are no longer necessarily followers of Jesus Christ.

To add to the confusion and the decay of the word, we have people who refer to themselves as Christians because of their family, church, or ethnic backgrounds, while they are in no way personally associated with Jesus Christ, and are neither knowledgeable nor concerned about what it means to follow him. Due to the vagueness of the word, it is quite easy to say, "Yes, of course I'm a Christian. I'm not a Hindu or a Muslim or anything else, so I guess I'm a Christian."

Contrast that widely accepted but muddied understanding of Christian with the phrase "Christ Follower." The latter is much clearer, more descriptive, and offers little wiggle room. It's not quite so easy to flippantly say, "I'm a Christ Follower" because of what it so obviously implies. Christ Follower—unlike Christian—doesn't define a caricature of a certain religion, it doesn't simply carve out a philosophical space within the wide spectrum of competing world religions. It's not about a culture or a country, or a framing of what one is not. A Christ Follower is a person who identifies with the One who possesses a widely known and widely respected reputation, teaching and way of life.

While there may be disagreement between Christians and Muslims and Jews and new-agers and atheists about exactly who Jesus is and what he did, in some cases whether he actually walked this earth or not, there is still a common sense of his character, his conduct, and his posture toward others. And so, if you were to say that the Roman Catholic Christ Followers were fighting against the Protestant Christ Followers in a certain part of the world, or that the Christ Followers in a certain country were hunting down and killing Muslims, or that the Hollywood Christ Followers were producing entertainment that glorified revenge and undermined every level of authority, it would sound completely ludicrous. Anyone who knows anything about the historical Jesus Christ knows that this type of conduct is certainly not a part of following him.

For the above reasons, this book isn't called *The DNA of a Christian*. And for the same reasons I rarely refer to myself as a Christian, but rather as a follower of Jesus Christ. In fact, in my more introspective moments, I might refer to myself as a "prospective follower of Jesus Christ" because I recognize that my following is still less than complete, that there are moments when my internal and external lives don't correspond with what it means to fully follow Jesus. Yes, we must always rest in the completed work of Jesus, knowing that we are covered by his righteousness, that we are "in him" and that it is by grace we have been saved through faith. But at the same time, if only for the sake of those watching from the outside seeking the truth, we mustn't pretend we are perfect in our following; they know we are not. The good news is that while they do expect a different type of conduct from Christ Followers, and while they crave a certain level of authenticity and honesty, they don't expect perfection.

How Do You Start Following Jesus?

Inside the North American Evangelical Christian subculture with which I am familiar, the way we "become a Christian" or "accept Jesus" feeds into and further emphasizes the Christian/Christ Follower distinction. Consider the life cycle of the common evangelical Christian:

Whether raised in a church-going home or not, a significant number of people, as children or teens, come to a concise understanding of who Jesus Christ is (God the Son, come in the flesh) and what he did (died on the cross to pay the price for our sins). Sometimes the motivating catalyst is the carrot (heaven) and sometimes it is the stick (hell). For many who responded in this way as I did at Bible camp in the early 1970s, as many others did in response to the Thief in the Night movie series, as still others did later in the mid-1990s in response to the Left Behind series the motivation was a fear of missing out on "the rapture" when Jesus would snatch away all true believers and leave everyone else behind.

A very common response to this fear is the praying of a prayer in which individuals "invite Jesus into their hearts." This phraseology seems to spring from Revelation 3.20: *"Here I am! I stand at the door and knock. If anyone hears my voice and opens the door, I will come in and eat with them and they with me."* But this passage was written to a church, to a group of people who were already Christians but who had drifted into what is described as a lukewarm state—they were following Jesus with less purity than they had in the past. It wasn't written to people who needed to begin following Jesus for the first time. This call to accept Jesus is often made following an "altar call" in which people come forward or stay behind after a church or camp or youth service. These altar calls are a rather recent development, having been invented, or at least popularized in the 1800s by evangelist Charles Finney.

Occasionally these young people are baptized, though many are not. Frequently they go through a rebellious stage marked by periodic "rededications" to Christ at camps or youth conferences. As they leave high school and move into the workforce or postsecondary education, many drift still further away from the church and Christianity. Some, upon getting married and having children, drift back, and some, by the grace of God, pick up where they left off and begin to learn what it means to follow Jesus Christ.

Regarding baptism, in the evangelical denomination I have been a part of most of my life, there have generally been twice as many conversions/professions of faith as baptisms, year after year after year. Given that Jesus described "making disciples" as baptizing someone and teaching them to obey his teaching, it seems plain that getting someone to pray a prayer is not the same thing as making a disciple.

What this all means is that we (North American Evangelicals) have often focused on making a certain kind of Christian that fits into our North American Evangelical subculture, but not on making disciples, true followers of Jesus Christ. Empirical data showing little if any measurable difference in the conduct of those who profess faith in Christ versus those who do not only reinforces this conclusion.

In contrast to this "pray a prayer and accept Jesus into your heart" methodology, the New Testament pattern seems less mystical and more concrete.

In Acts 2, following the outpouring of the Holy Spirit, Peter preaches a very direct message to those gathered in Jerusalem, and the crowd, under great conviction asks, "'*Brothers, what shall we do?*' *Peter replied, 'Repent and be baptized, every one of you, in the name of Jesus Christ, for the forgiveness of your sins.*'" (Acts 2.38)

In Acts 16, following an earthquake and a near suicide attempt, the Philippian jailer asks "'*Sirs, what must I do to be saved?*' *They replied, 'Believe in the Lord Jesus, and you will be saved, you and your household.*'" (Acts 16.30-31) Following some first aid for the wounds Paul and Silas had received from their flogging, "*...immediately he and all his household were baptized.*" (Acts 16.33)

Romans 10 describes the word of faith that Paul and his ministry team proclaimed as this: "*If you declare with your mouth 'Jesus is Lord,' and believe in your heart that God raised him from the dead, you will be saved.*" (Romans 10.9)

John 1.12 says "*Yet to all who did receive him, to those who believed on his name, he gave the right to become children of God...*"

There are many more passages we could look at to gather further data and nuance, but the bottom line answer to the question of how a person becomes a Christian in the biblical sense, how a person begins to follow Jesus Christ, is through repentance and faith, demonstrated in baptism. To put it another way, converts in the early church didn't "pray a prayer" to accept Jesus, they responded to the Gospel with repentance and faith, and their first act of following Jesus was baptism. In a sense, baptism was their prayer, their act of repentance and faith. There was no altar call, there was a water call.

Please don't misunderstand what I am saying. I am NOT saying that all those who respond to the Gospel with a prayer aren't saved, aren't Christians. If there is repentance and faith they are. And I'm certainly not saying that it is the act of baptism alone that saves. I am simply saying that as far as I can tell, the biblical pattern to begin following Jesus Christ is a response to who he is and what he has done, a response of repentance and faith (both of which are, by the way, gifts or works of the Holy Spirit in a person's life) made visible through baptism. Passages that seem to hint at the physical act of baptism bestowing salvation (Acts 22.16, 1 Peter 2.21) must be seen in the larger New Testament context which shows that water baptism is an act of repentance and faith in response to the gospel. "Baptism saves" only to the extent that it is accompanied by, and is an expression of, repentance and faith.

In short, the New Testament answer to the question of "What must I do to be saved? How do I become a Christian? What is the first step in following Jesus?" is "Repent of your sins, believe in Jesus Christ, and as your first act of repentance, faith, obedience and following, get baptized."

If we became Christians in this way, with a solid repentance and faith, reinforced in short order by the obedient act of baptism, we would actually start down the path of being "Christ Followers" as well. The two terms would again be synonymous, the traits discussed in the following pages would be more prevalent within the people of our churches, and the effectiveness of the Church in contributing to the coming of the Kingdom would grow dramatically.

Section II

The Traits

CHAPTER 3

Lover of God

"Teacher, which is the greatest commandment in the Law?" Jesus replied, "'Love the Lord your God with all your heart and with all your soul and with all your mind.' This is the first and greatest commandment."
(Matthew 22.36-38)

I n the late 1970s when I was in my early teens I went on a canoe trip with the boy's group my father led in association with our church. It was the perfect trip for a bunch of junior high students with too much energy: Large lakes with strong winds and rough water, a small river with challenging but not dangerous rapids, rugged campsites, and lots of fish. My friends and I talked about it for years afterward.

One cool, early morning as we paddled across a perfectly calm, glassy lake smattered with a maze of islands, mist rising off the water, my dad broke the silent spell and began to sing one of his favorite hymns:

O Lord my God! When I in awesome wonder
Consider all the worlds thy hands have made,
I see the stars, I hear the rolling thunder,

Thy power throughout the universe displayed.
Then sings my soul, my Saviour God to Thee.
How great Thou art, how great Thou art!...[1]

Actually, to say he "sang" the song is to use the term loosely—he was never known for his musical ability and was fond of saying "The Bible says 'Make a joyful noise.' Doesn't say it has to be pretty!"

As he sang that morning, his words boomed and rolled across the water. Apart from the steady stroking and light splashes of our paddles, it was the only sound. All of the guys, 90% of whom were not from a Christian background, looked around at each other as if to say, "What's going on? This is a bit weird." I was more than a little embarrassed. I'd never seen him do anything quite like that before, outside of a church service. I kept my eyes forward, paddling hard, trying to somehow pretend "I don't know that man!"

Yet, since my father passed away from cancer on a Christmas Eve more than twenty years ago, that moment has become one of the snapshots in my mind of what he was like. As with every earthly father, he was far from perfect. But he did have a love for God that often surfaced when he was outdoors. At that moment in time on the misty lake, surrounded by the lavish artwork of His Creator, he was so filled with joy at seeing God's creation, so filled with love for Him, that he had to sing. It simply burst out of him.

A Christ Follower is a Lover of God. This is the first of the eight DNA markers and is a character quality so obvious it can almost go unstated. After all, it is based on the single greatest commandment as identified by Jesus Christ himself. Yes, a primary character quality of Christ Followers is that they love God. And everyone says, "Amen!" and goes home. Who can argue with loving God? But the real question, the real issue as with all of the character qualities addressed in this book is, "What in the world does it mean?!? What does that look like? How do I get it, show it, live it?" Put another

---

1   *How Great Thou Art*, © 1953, Stewart Hine, Assigned To Manna Music

way, "How do you know if you love God?" Or, "How do you know how much you love God?"

I once sat with four other pastors, each from a different theological background and discussed this question. We agreed on so many things, but there was a surprising lack of clarity when it came to finding consensus on what it means and looks like to love God. One of the difficulties with getting a grasp on the issue of loving God is that he is invisible and physically untouchable. It's not like you can say, "If you love God give him a big hug."

What does it mean to love God? How would you measure your love for God? Do you raise your hands in worship? Maybe we can measure love for God by the raising of our hands. Those who get them way up there really love God. Those who are kind of in the middle, chest high hand lifters like me, reluctantly demonstrative worshipers, are lukewarm, sort-of lovers of God. Which would mean that those who never raise their hands in worship are spiritually cold, they obviously don't love God. Of course not! Despite the fact that animation in worship has been presented by some as a measurement tool for love of God it is a false metric.

Perhaps we could evaluate our love for God by tracking the minutes and hours we spend in the Word and prayer. That's a nice concrete measure. Perhaps unless you're at one hour plus daily, you are just not a very good lover of God. As with hand-raising, devotional time is, in fact, sometimes viewed as a measure for love of God or spiritual maturity—at least by those who put in the time!

Then there are the dollars given to the right causes, souls saved through our evangelistic efforts, the number of cinder block churches we've helped build in third world countries...and on it goes. Unfortunately, amazingly, all of these have been proposed, explicitly or implicitly, by some people as measures of our love for God.

So how DO you measure, or at least evaluate, love? It is the foundational character quality of a Christ Follower. But unless we can make it more tangible, more concrete, it is very difficult to address and develop in our lives.

There certainly are significant benefits promised to lovers of God: preservation and protection (Psalm 31.23, 145.20); intimacy with Him (John 14.23, 1 Corinthians 8.3); God's work for good in all circumstances (Romans 8.28); an unimaginable rich destiny (1 Corinthians 2.9); the crown of life (James 1.12). If only there was a way to measure and evaluate our love for God.

Well, maybe there is.

> *Psalm 5.11 says, "But let all who take refuge in you be glad; let them ever sing for joy. Spread your protection over them, that those who love your name may rejoice in you." The old KJV says, "...let them also that love thy name be joyful in thee." And the NASB says, "... that those who love thy name may exult in thee."[2]*

I like that word "exult." It is a rich word that captures a heart-felt, passionate, full-bodied joy that cannot help but overflow. You've likely seen it, as I have, in people coming out of the water following their baptisms, or in a child opening a gift to discover it's "just what I always wanted!" You may recall as I do, the day in July, 2013 when Andy Murray became the first men's singles Wimbledon champion for Britain in 77 years. You can easily find the video online of his hard fought final winning point, game and set to take the match from Novak Djokovic, the top ranked player in the world at the time. His response and the response of his countrymen is one of the best illustrations I've seen of this idea of overflowing joy and exuberance.

"That those who love your name may rejoice (exult) in you." (Ps 5.11). Exulting, worshipping, basking in his presence. This rejoicing, this worship is a sign of love for God, just as the ability of two people to snuggle quietly in front of a fire or walk hand in hand down a beach, enjoying each other's presence is an indication of love for each other.

---

2   Scripture Taken From *The New American Sandard Bible,* © 1960, 1962, 1963, 1968, 1971, 1972, 1973, 1975, 1977, By The Lockman Foundation. Used By Permission.

A Lover of God is a Worshipper of God

A Christ Follower is a lover of God. And a lover of God is a worshipper of God. This isn't talking about mere singing, but worship. So much has been written and taught on worship in recent years that most of us now understand the difference between words and worship, the difference between music and worship. Matt Redman's song "The Heart of Worship" is a prime example of this broader understanding of worship. Romans 12.1-2 describes worship as a total offering of ourselves back to him, as a response to his great mercy toward us and all creation. I often refer to this offering of ourselves as the "heart and the start of worship." It is the start of worship because until we do that, no matter how much we sing or serve or do other Christian-y things, we have not worshipped. And it is the heart of worship because if we offer ourselves to him completely, we have worshipped in the fullest possible way. All the other expressions of worship—service, singing, giving—naturally flow from this self-offering.

Do you ever exult in God, rejoice in God? Does your heart ever boil over in worship to him as my father's did on that morning lake? This kind of body-soul-spirit, total-person response to him in worship is one indication that you are a lover God.

Loving God Goes Beyond Emotions

But because this exulting has such a strong emotional component, we're not always there. At least I'm not always there. My father wasn't always there. King David, the prime example of worship in scripture, wasn't always there. Sometimes he didn't exult in God, sometimes he couldn't exult in God because it seemed like God wasn't present. But he still loved God. So beyond this exultation, this overflow of worship, how do we measure and evaluate and grow in our love for God?

When I first dug into this topic I read every reference in the Bible about love. A good number of them talk about loving God.

Seventeen of those references say essentially the same thing, and give us a clue as to how we can love God and how we know if we are loving God, even if we aren't in that glow of exultation. It's rather easy to spot when you cluster some of the passages together, beginning in the Old Testament:

> "And now, O Israel, what does the Lord your God
> ask of you but to fear the Lord your God, to walk
> in obedience to him, to love him, to serve the Lord
> your God with all your heart and with all your soul,
> and to observe the Lord's commands and decrees
> that I am giving you today for your own good?"
> (Deuteronomy 10.12-13)

> "Love the Lord your God and keep his requirements,
> his decrees, his laws and his commands always."
> (Deuteronomy 11.1)

> "Let those who love the Lord hate evil..." (Psalm
> 97.10)

Look at the continuity with New Testament passages:

Jesus, speaking in the Gospel of John says "If you love me, keep my commands." (John 14.15)

And finally, the Apostle of Love himself put it this way: "In fact, this is love for God: to keep his commands..." (1 John 5.3)

Do you see it? What is the answer to the question of what it means to love God?

In his foundational book on this subject, Loving God, Charles Colson tells the story of a young married mom in Washington who surprised her church by sharing how just a few years previously she had been living a double life of sexual activity and drug use, while still being quite active in church life. She found herself pregnant and was being pressured toward abortion when she decided it was time to follow Jesus regardless of the cost. She shared, "I was still everything I never wanted to be—pregnant, alone, deserted by family, and *rejected by the one I had loved. Yet for the first time in my life I was really peaceful, because I knew for the first time in my life I was being obedient.*[3]

Loving God Means Obeying God

How do you measure love for God? How do you know if you are a lover of God? From cover to cover in the Bible, the answer is the same: Loving God means obeying God. A Christ Follower is a lover of God. And a lover of God obeys God. Love for God is revealed in obedience to God. And that is somewhat measurable isn't it? To ask, "Do you love God?" is to ask, at least in part, "Do you obey God?" This gives an uncharacteristic concreteness to one of the fuzziest concepts in the English language.

Yet just as we don't always exult in God, we don't always obey God. And even our moments of obedience are often tainted by questionable motives. James says *"We all stumble in many ways."* (3.2) So...where does that leave us?

First, we need to be honest and admit that based on the clear scriptural link between loving God and obeying him, when we disobey—either as an event or in an ongoing way—that disobedience truly indicates a lack of love for the Lord.

Second, we need to recognize that the issue isn't being perfectly obedient all the time. If that were the case, we would be forced to conclude that none of us loves God in the least.

I find it helpful in times of self-evaluation, and even in mentoring others, to think in terms of trajectory: Is the trajectory of my life one of increasing obedience? Do I have a walk of obedience interspersed with stumbles and disobediences, rather than a walk of disobedience interspersed with moments of obedience? Is my life one of consistent, persevering obedience to him even when I feel lousy, even when those around me are not living in obedience, even when others don't want me to obey him? Or am I a "chameleon Christian,"

---

3   Charles Colson, *Loving God*, Hardcover Edition, Grand Rapids: Zondervan, 138-39)

taking on the practices of those around me—a great Christ Follower when surrounded by Christ Followers, and a great sinner when surrounded by sinners? I believe it is that trajectory of obedience, that growth in obedience, which marks a lover of God.

By that measure are you a lover of God? By that measure, how much do you love God?

Those are important evaluative questions, but don't park on them for too long.

There is a great danger for people who begin to grapple with this issue of loving God, that they will follow this hazardous line of logic:

1. A Christ Follower is a lover of God. And that would be true.

2. Loving God means obeying God. And that would also be true.

3. Therefore I need to work really hard to obey God and prove my love for him. And that would be false, or at best, incomplete.

The application of the truth that loving God means obeying God is not, "Try real hard to obey God and prove your love for him." It is something far more revolutionary and much more liberating.

There's an old story of a woman who found herself married to a nasty, abusive, dictatorial man. So controlling was he that he took the time to write out a comprehensive list of chores and rules and duties for her to follow. Even though she genuinely tried to fulfill his demands and please him, she could never measure up to the list. In time, he died, and eventually the woman remarried. The man she married was the polar opposite of her first husband. He was kind and generous and loved her unconditionally. Several years into this marriage, the woman stumbled upon the old list from her former slave-driver of a husband. And to her shock, she discovered that she was actually doing everything on his list for her new husband. And not only was she doing it all, she was doing it easily, freely, joyfully.

In Ps 116.1 it says, *"I love the Lord, for he heard my voice; he heard my cry for mercy."* The Lord reminded his people through Jeremiah, *"I have loved you with an everlasting love; I have drawn you with unfailing kindness."* (Jeremiah 31.3)

The most memorized verse in the Bible says, *"For God so loved the world that he gave his one and only Son..."* Romans 2.4 tells us that *"God's kindness is intended to lead you to repentance."* Romans 5.8 continues with *"But God demonstrates his own love for us in this: While we were still sinners, Christ died for us."*

Ephesians 2.4-5 adds, *"But because of his great love for us, God, who is rich in mercy, made us alive with Christ even when we were dead in transgressions—it is by grace you have been saved."*

And once again the apostle John in his textbook on love caps it off with, *"This is love: not that we loved God, but that he loved us and sent his Son as an atoning sacrifice for our sins."* (1 John 4.10)

Loving God is Initiated by God

Here's the point that we must not miss: The source of our love for God is not our own energy or determination. It is not something we drum up on the inside and concentrate on and work hard at. The source of our love for God is God's love for us! It is critically important to grasp this truth. The way we grow in our love for God is not by exerting tremendous effort and concentration to obey him and prove our love. The way we grow in our love for God, our exultation of God, our worship and obedience of God, is by growing in our understanding, acceptance, and experience of God's love for us.

There is another extremely crucial point in this question of how we can love God. Jesus reveals a profound truth with some deceptively simple words in John 15 and 17: *"As the Father has loved me, so have I loved you. Now remain in my love. If you keep my commands, you will remain in my love, just as I have kept my Father's commands and remain in his love."* (John 15.9-10)

> *"My prayer is not for them alone. I pray also for those who will believe in me through their message, that all of them may be one, Father, just as you are in me and I am in you. May they also be in us so that the world may believe that you have sent me. I have given them*

*the glory that you gave me, that they may be one as
we are one—I in them and you in me—so that they
may be brought to complete unity. Then the world will
know that you sent me and have loved them even as
you have loved me." (John 17.20-23)*

Do you see the progression? In John 15 we see that as the Father
loves Jesus, Jesus loves us, and as Jesus has obeyed and remained in
the Father's love, we can obey Jesus and remain in his love. In John
17 we see that the oneness of believers is to mirror the oneness of
the Father and Son, and that the Father loves us as he loves the Son.

What is happening in these excerpts (which are just a tiny representation of the vast panorama of John 14-17) is that we—all
believers—are being invited into the love relationship of the Trinity
as participants. We are not merely spectators of this love, we are
included in it, we are given the opportunity to "abide" in this flow
of perfect love.

The invitation to abide, to participate in this love relationship is
not merely a call to an intellectual affirmation, but rather a call to
a mysterious, supernatural experience that transcends our mental
capacities. Hence the prayer of Paul in Ephesians 3.17-19: *"And
I pray that you, being rooted and established in love, may have power,
together with all the Lord's people, to grasp how wide and long and high
and deep is the love of Christ, and to know this love that surpasses knowledge—that you may be filled to the measure of all the fullness of God."*

In what is seen by some as an "evangel-legend," but as far as I
have been able to determine is based on a real event, theologian
Karl Barth was asked the following question at one of his lectures
in the eastern United States in 1962: "What is the most profound
thought that you know, Dr. Barth?" His response: "Jesus loves me,
this I know, for the Bible tells me so."

The fact of God's unconditional love for us is one of the greatest
biblical truths and yet one of the most difficult for us to absorb. Why
is that? It's at least in part because unconditional love is extremely
rare. Many people never experience it, so when they hear of God's

amazing love for them it is unprecedented, and hence suspect. Even those of us who were blessed with stable Christian homes and loving parents can often think of moments when our parents responded to us unfairly or in some other way gave an indication that their love was less than absolutely unconditional, even if it wasn't. As a husband and parent now myself, I believe that I love my wife and two children unconditionally, yet I sometimes catch myself treating them in ways that are something less than unconditionally loving.

To further muddy the water, due to our limited perspective, it sometimes seems like God isn't treating us as we think he would if he really did love us unconditionally. Yet he does, always. If there was ever an area where we need to apply the Romans 12.2 directive *"...be transformed by the renewing of your mind"* it is here. We need to allow the rich biblical testimony of God's love for us to soak into our hearts. We need to allow ourselves to receive it, bask in it, exult in it, absorb it. And as we grow in the joyful rest of knowing his love for us, our love for him, our obedience to him will blossom.

"This is love: not that we loved God, but that he loved us..." And when I know God loves me, when I understand what Jesus did for me, when I catch a glimpse of God's heart toward me, I will at times burst open with worship of him, I will at other times sit in silent awe, the trend line of my life will be one of obedience to him, I will love him. And it won't be the battle it so often is in my life. *"In fact, this is love for God: to keep his commands. And his commands are not burdensome..."* (1 John 5.3)

We are wise not to believe or accept all the praise we receive, not to let it go to our heads. But there is a danger that we will take this same approach with God's heart toward us and not let it go to our heads, when in fact we must! We must soak in it, live in it, exult in it, allow it to change us.

Loving God Requires Receiving God's Love

The application of this chapter, this look at the first aspect of the DNA of a Christ Follower is not, "Get out there and work at loving

God!" The application is, "Open up and receive his love." Open up and receive his love. That is the foundation of love for God, of obedience to God. As an aside, it is also the cornerstone of biblical self-esteem—to know that the one who made you and knows everything about you, good and bad, loves you beyond measure.

In recent years, the compilation of biblical truths by Barry Adams in *The Father's Love Letter* has been used by God to open up many hearts to the powerful concept that we have a Heavenly Father who planned us and knows us and wants a relationship with us. That might be a good place to start if you sense that you are weak in this basic character quality of loving God.

Have you received the Father's love for you, ever? God proved his love for you and I by sending Jesus Christ to die and pay the price for all the wrong things we have ever done or will ever do. The Bible says in John 1.12, *"Yet to all who did receive him, to those who believed in his name, he gave the right to become children of God..."*

Perhaps you need to start here, with a simple little communique from you to God:

"God, I know that you love me. I want to receive your love. I am sorry that I have done many wrong things. I turn from all my wrong doing, from my way of living to yours. I accept the fact that Jesus died for me. I receive him, I receive your love, I receive your forgiveness."

Reading those words does nothing. Saying them likewise means nothing. But making them yours, coming to the place where your heart is aligned with those words opens up the door of your life to the Father's love. If you could sign your name to those words with integrity, you have received him, you have believed in his name. When you do that, there are some further steps that will help you immensely. First, tell someone you know what you have done. The act of speaking it out will help lock in your response to God and may encourage them in their spiritual walk. Second, plug into a group of likeminded Christ Followers who can encourage you and walk with you in this new way of living. Third, get baptized. This is the biblical response, a physical demonstration of the heart intent captured in that little prayer above, that you are responding to God's love for you. In fact, baptism has been described as "the first act of obedience" of a Christ Follower, the idea being that we are dying to our own way of living and setting a pattern of obeying the Lord whenever he makes something clear to us. (See the previous chapter for more on this.)

Most likely, however, if you are reading these words, you have already accepted Jesus Christ as your Saviour. You have repented of your sins and put your faith in him, you're confident of your eternal destiny with him. But when you look at yourself honestly, it may be that you see your love has grown cold. You may sing, but you don't worship, you don't offer yourself to him unreservedly. You rarely exult in him. There is very little overflow of his love displayed in you. You may live a decidedly moral life, serving him faithfully, but in some areas you are knowingly, consistently disobedient to him.

Repentance, a change of mind leading to a change of action, making that 180-degree turn from our way of living to his way of living, is always a part of the answer when we have wandered from him. But remember, it's God's kindness that moves us to repentance (Romans 2.4) and his love that moves us to obedience, and his love that moves us to worship. So the answer for you if you find yourself in that cooled-off state is the same as the answer for someone who has not yet come to Jesus for the first time: Open up and receive his love.

Growing as a Lover of God

Here are some suggestions on how to begin, or continue, to do that.

1. Get on your knees and get your hands open palms up. (Never underestimate the link between our physical posture and internal heart posture!) Personalize some of the love passages we looked at earlier:

   "I love you Lord for you heard my voice, you heard my cry for mercy." (Psalm 116.1)

*"You have loved me with an everlasting love; you have
drawn me with unfailing kindness."* (Jeremiah 31.3)
*"You demonstrated your own love for me in this: While
I was still a sinner, Christ died for me."* (Romans 5.8)

Perhaps there are other passages or scripture-based songs you
know that resonate with your heart. Personalize them in prayer
as well. Think of all the indications, biblical and personal, that
you see of his love for you. Thank him for each one. Then personalize Romans 12.1: "In view of all your great mercies to me I
offer my body to you as a living sacrifice, which is my reasonable
response of worship to you."

2. Pray for God to enable you to receive his love, to unlock your
   love receptors. I know from experience that unprocessed pain
   from our past and from hurtful relationships can be a hindrance
   to receiving his love. Pray for the ability to grasp the amazing
   truth that you are unconditionally loved by your Creator. Read
   Paul's prayer for you in Ephesians 3.17-19: *"And I pray that you,
   being rooted and established in love, may have power, together with all
   the Lord's people, to grasp how wide and long and high and deep is the
   love of Christ, and to know this love that surpasses knowledge..."* Ask
   God for that to happen in you, for you to somehow know and
   experience the unknowable, unfathomable love of the Father.

3. Have others pray for you. There may be very specific situations
   from your past that can make it difficult to accept God's love for
   you. God is not like anyone else. Don't define the love of your
   Heavenly Father by how others have treated you. Let his Word,
   the Bible, define his love. And let those who love you and love
   Him put their hands on you and pray for the breakthrough you
   may need. So much of what the Lord Jesus wants to do in us he
   does in the context of his community, the church.

4. Get baptized. If you haven't been baptized as a believer, the
   physical act of baptism is a significant offering of yourself to him.
   Baptism is an act of obedience, which as we have seen means

that it is also an act of love. If you are what I refer to as a "dry Christian," get baptized as soon as you can!

5. Soak in the passages of scripture that speak of God's love for you. Many have been listed in this chapter. You can easily find others with a concordance or by simply starting to read in Psalms or the New Testament. Let his word be a hammer and sword and a fire, smashing, penetrating and burning your heart with his love.

———————

A Christ Follower is a lover of God, a person who, having experienced God's love, is moved to respond in worship and unconditional obedience.

———————

CHAPTER 4

Lover of People

*"Teacher, which is the greatest commandment in the
Law?" Jesus replied, "'Love the Lord your God with
all your heart and with all your soul and with all your
mind.' This is the first and greatest commandment.
And the second is like it: 'Love your neighbor as yourself.' All the Law and the Prophets hang on these two
commandments." (Matthew 22.36-40)*

"He's got a loaded handgun to his head right now! What do I do?!?" Her voice was urgent and terrified.

"Are you sure it's loaded?" I asked.

"Yes, I heard him load it over the phone just before I called you. I don't think he's joking."

I took a deep breath. If he wasn't joking, we needed to act now. Yet, if he wasn't suicidal, but simply trying to manipulate his wife into getting back together with him, and we got the police involved, there could be serious consequences. I made a decision.

"Call the police," I said. "I'll head over to his place right now." I raced across town toward my friend's suite. But just before I got to his neighborhood I met a police car coming the other direction, with him sitting in the back.

As it turned out, and as I had suspected, he wasn't suicidal at all. He was shocked when the police arrived and confiscated his pistol along with his other firearms. In the end, my friend who was a hunting fanatic and one of the few people I enjoyed going into the wilderness with, lost his guns, and by extension, his hunting privileges for a number of years. As his marriage had struggled and then moved into a legal separation, hunting had been his route of escape, one of his few unadulterated pleasures. Now it was gone, and I was in some measure responsible. Had I, in one of the toughest snap decisions I have ever had to make, done right by my friend? Had I acted in a loving way?

A Christ Follower is a lover of God, a person who, experiencing God's love, is moved to respond in worship and unconditional obedience. But the love doesn't end there. In Matthew 22, Jesus says the second greatest command is "Love your neighbor as yourself." So, in addition to being a lover of God, a Christ Follower is also a lover of people. But what exactly does it mean to love people, both in the ordinary grind of life and in challenging situations like the one recounted above?

Before we explore what it means to be a lover of people, and take a look at the motivation for doing so, it's helpful to underscore how relevant this issue is in our season of history.

Loving People Will Become a Rarity

In Matthew 24, Jesus is responding to his disciples' questions about the destruction of Jerusalem, and the sign of his coming and the end of the age. He speaks about the rise of false prophets and false messiahs, and the well-known "birth pains" of wars, famines, and earth quakes. Continuing on with his response he says,

> *"Then you will be handed over to be persecuted and put to death, and you will be hated by all nations because of me. At that time many will turn away from the faith and will betray and hate each other, and many false prophets will appear and deceive many people. Because of the increase of wickedness, the love of most will grow cold..." (Matthew 24.9-12)*

As this age progresses toward its culmination, "the love of most will grow cold." A very similar statement is made in 2 Timothy about the last days:

> "But mark this: There will be terrible times in the last days. People will be lovers of themselves, lovers of money, boastful, proud, abusive, disobedient to their parents, ungrateful, unholy, without love, unforgiving, slanderous, without self-control, brutal, not lovers of the good, treacherous, rash, conceited, lovers of pleasure rather than lovers of God—having a form of godliness but denying its power." (2 Timothy 3.1-5)

There is a lot of "love" in that passage: love for self, love for money, love for pleasure…but notably no love for God. And, in relation to other people, the statement is simply "without love." In the last days people who love other people will be rare.

Followers of Jesus Christ are called to be, in character, at the core of who they are, lovers of people. Yet scripture warns us that it is going to be increasingly difficult to fulfill that calling in the days before Christ's return due to the degeneration of society. The pull of gravity will be, and already is, away from being a lover of people.

An indication that we are at least moving in that direction is something I have been aware of my entire Christian life, but have seen with greater frequency since beginning pastoral ministry in 1990. I have discovered that for many Christ Followers this character quality is not a nonnegotiable. It is not seen as an essential part of their DNA. Too frequently I have come across people who claim to be followers of Jesus Christ, people who would claim to be and, indeed, look like lovers of God—passionate worshippers, who are involved in a church—but who have a decided lack of love for other people. Unforgiveness is savored, and in some cases visible hatred of others is openly expressed. Blogs and other social media sites are full of comments from Christians condemning other Christians for slight variations of theology, often on secondary and tertiary issues.

It seems that our love for others is often predicated on their total agreement with our opinions.

We can laugh at one ministry couple's description of their congregation that was so nasty "It wasn't actually a church; it was a group of mean people who got together on Sunday mornings"[4] and yet the implications of that kind of "church" is terrifying. Even scarier is the question of whether you or I have ever been one of those mean people. I know that, at times, I have found myself slipping into the spiritual contradiction of loving God, but not people. Yet as we will see, scripture doesn't allow us to separate the two.

The Austin Lounge Lizards have a song called *Jesus Loves Me (But He Can't Stand You)*. It is a cynical observation of the inconsistency of claiming to love God and follow Jesus, but not love people:

> *I know you smoke, I know you drink that brew*
> *I just can't abide a sinner like you*
> *God can't either, that's why I know it to be true that*
> *Jesus loves me—but he can't stand you*
> *I'm going to heaven, boys, when I die*
> *'Cause I've crossed every "t" and I've dotted every "i"*
> *My preacher tells me that I'm God's kind of guy; that's why*
> *Jesus loves me—but you're gonna fry...*[5]

And on the song goes, viciously pillorying Christians and churches that claim to be lovers of God, but not lovers of people. Why is it so obvious to those outside the church that this posture, even in its less graphic but all too common manifestations, is hypocritical and indefensible? It is logically and biblically absurd to think we can be on track with God and yet fail to love people. Jesus himself said that being a lover of people is an essential character quality. It is to be a part of our DNA. But it's hard. So how can we actually

---

4   Dean Merrill, Clergy Couples in Crisis, Carol Stream: CTi, 1985, 15-16
5   Austin Lounge Lizards, *Jesus Loves Me (But He Can't Stand You)*, Lizard Vision, 1991

do it? What is the motivation and where do we get the capacity for loving people?

Some people are just loveable; it takes no effort. The most natural thing is to love them. They are teddy bears, grandmotherly or grandfatherly. There are people like that in every church, every neighborhood, perhaps every political party—even the ones I will never vote for! But then there are those other people—sandpaper people, EGR's (extra grace required), thorns in the flesh, those people whom it is not natural to love. It often hurts to love them, it costs to love them, and yet we are, seemingly impossibly, called to love them.

Many years ago I came across a story in a newspaper describing a woman killed in a hit and run accident in Rio de Janeiro. Despite the city's high homicide rate at the time, which created a general numbness to violence, the accident report landed on the front page. As the woman attempted to cross a busy highway near a beachside neighborhood, she was struck and killed. But no one stopped. The cars kept coming, driving over her again and again, for hours. By the time a recovery was attempted neither the race nor approximate age of the woman could be determined.

When I first read that clipping it shocked me, and it still does today. But what bothers me most, apart from the vivid picture of brutal inhumanity it has painted in my mind, is that it is not really an isolated incident. It is a snapshot of the value placed on human life in our world today. And I'm not just talking about the kind of butchering that happens "over there." It seems that everywhere you look on this planet, people are seen as expendable commodities. They are hired, milked for the best years of their lives, and then let go. They are used for unloving sensual pleasure. They are enslaved. They are aborted. They are considered collateral damage in military strikes. They are seen as, and sometimes even called, "trash".

I experienced a very small taste of what those on the fringes of society face, when as a student in the Arrow Leadership Program I was assigned to dress up like a street person and panhandle for ten dollars. I chose to go into the wealthy, oil industry city of Edmonton,

Alberta on a windy twenty-below-zero winter morning to fulfill the requirements of the assignment. I'd prepared by not shaving for several days, and added to the disguise by digging out my old "bush clothes"—a ratty, plaid-colored wool jacket and some well-worn work pants. I added a dark dirty toque and sunglasses for good measure.

As I took my place along the sidewalk in front of a large electronics store, I thought the biting cold would make my task easier. I was wrong. I quickly learned how much people can communicate with their eyes. When you are begging for money, the act itself is humiliating. It's very easy to feel, well, like dirt. And the treatment you receive from people only reinforces that feeling. Not all the people were hostile and uncaring, some were visibly kind and compassionate—though not to the point of giving me any money. But most just had a way of looking at me and somehow communicating silently with a glance, through narrowed eyes and slightly curled lips, "You are an inconvenience, an eyesore. You are the equivalent of a piece of litter on the sidewalk."

After about twenty minutes, a young manager from the electronics store, flanked by two husky assistants came marching out and informed me (in more graphic language than I will share) that my presence was bothering some of the customers, and that I better leave. They then marched behind me across the parking lot until I was well away from their store. Their aggressive posture actually scared me and I felt like any resistance on my part would lead to a physical altercation.

The entire experience challenged me to some serious introspection. I had to ask myself if I valued people based on how they look, how they dress, and on whether or not they appear to be holding down a decent job. The conversation with myself was not entirely pleasant.

We Love People Because They Have Inherent Value

When you see Jesus reaching out to those ostracized by society and the religious establishment of his day, when you read that God created us in his image—every single one of us—when you understand that every person you will ever see is going to live forever somewhere, when you look at the sweep of teaching in scripture about people, you discover that unlike our scaled value system, in God's eyes people have an inherent, priceless, eternal value.

Do you believe it? People have inherent eternal value. People have value apart from any beauty, accomplishment, net worth, work skills, intelligence or personality. They have inherent value. And that is at least the start of why we are called to love them. They're not like a car that finally stops and is broken up for parts. They are not like a pet that dies and is gone forever. They are eternal beings with an inherent, priceless value, and because of this we must love them. They are the most valuable things we will ever lay eyes on while we walk this planet.

But this is not the only reason to love others. There is another more direct and unavoidable impetus to love people in general and each other in particular. Look at these verses from 1 John:

*"For this is the message you heard from the beginning:
We should love one another." (3.11)*

*"We know that we have passed from death to life,
because we love each other. Anyone who does not love
remains in death." (3.14)*

*"This is how we know what love is: Jesus Christ laid
down his life for us. And we ought to lay down our
lives for one another." (3.16)*

*"And this is his command: to believe in the name of
his Son, Jesus Christ, and to love one another as he
commanded us." (3.23)*

*"Dear friends, let us love one another, for love comes
from God. Everyone who loves has been born of God*

and knows God. Whoever does not love does not know God, because God is love." (4.7-8)

"Dear Friends, since God so loved us, we also ought to love one another. No one has ever seen God; but if we love one another, God lives in us and his love is made complete in us." (4.11-12)

"And so we know and rely on the love God has for us. God is love. Whoever lives in love lives in God, and God in them." (4.16)

"If we say we love God yet hate a brother or sister, we are liars. For if we do not love a fellow believer, whom we have seen, we cannot love God, whom we have not seen. And he has given us this command: Those who love God must also love one another." (4.20-21)

We Love People as an Extension of Our Love for God

According to these verses, loving people is an extension of, and proof of, our love for God. Loving people is an aspect of loving God. More than that, loving people is one of the visible markers that we love God.

"We love because he first loved us." Park on that thought for a few seconds. We saw in the previous chapter that our love for God is a response to his love for us: We love him because he loves us. But with people it's different: We love them, not because they love us. They may not. We love them because He loves them, because the One we follow loves them and gave himself for them.

Think of a good friend, someone you have truly come to love. When you meet someone who is part of their family or another friend of theirs, you experience an immediate bond between yourself and that new person because of your love for your friend. You love them, in some measure, because your friend loves them. So it is with being a lover of people: We love them because our Lord loves them. Love for people is an extension of and, in fact, a proof of our love for God.

Hebrews 6.10 says that God "...*will not forget your work and the love you have shown him as you have helped his people and continue to help them.*" Here we see a clear link drawn between loving God and helping/serving/loving his people.

The parable of the sheep and goats in Matthew 25 puts it in stark, unavoidable terms: "'*Truly I tell you, whatever you did for one of the least of these brothers and sisters of mine, you did for me.*'" (25.40) Then a few verses later, "*...whatever you did not do for one of the least of these, you did not do for me.*" (25.45)

Understanding what it means to love people is one level of the challenge. Another level is putting that knowledge into action, making it concrete:

> "*If any one of you has material possessions and sees a brother or sister in need but has no pity on them, how can the love of God be in you? Dear children, let us not love with words or tongue but with actions and in truth.*" (1 John 3.17-18)

The ultimate challenge in loving people is loving those who don't love us, who are, in fact, our enemies. As Jesus said in the Sermon on the Mount,

> "*You have heard that it was said, 'Love your neighbor and hate your enemy.' But I tell you, love your ene-mies and pray for those who persecute you, that you may be children of your Father in heaven.*" (Matthew 5.43-45).

Jesus goes on to highlight how loving those who love us is no great accomplishment—everyone already does that. What gives his teaching here such power in the lives of his followers is the fact that he did exactly what he called us to: he loved his enemies, he wept over those who were opposed to him, he called out for their forgiveness right from the cross. Peter sums it up by saying, *"To this (suffering for good) you were called, because Christ suffered for you, leaving you an example, that you should follow in his steps. 'He committed no sin, and no deceit was found in his mouth.' When they hurled their insults at him, he did not retaliate; when he suffered, he made no threats. Instead, he entrusted himself to him who judges justly."* (1 Peter 2.21-23)

How much more clearly could it be stated? Following Jesus includes choosing to not retaliate against our enemies, to not threaten them, but to actually love them.

Learning to Love

So, what does it mean to love people—enemies or otherwise? How do you actually love? There is an old story about a psychology professor who always had ready parenting advice for his neighbors, especially when the children were being scolded or disciplined. He would always challenge the parents to love their children, not punish them. One hot day when he had just finished some cement work in his driveway, his little boy walked to the side of it and put down his foot to make a footprint. The professor ran over to the boy yelling, and was about to smack him on the bottom, when a neighbor leaned out the window and said, "Remember professor, love your child!" The professor hollered back, "I do love him, in the abstract. But not in the concrete!"

And that, of course, is the challenge—loving one another not merely with an idealized, theoretical, abstract love, but in all of their, and our, concrete unlovable-ness and imperfection. What does it mean to love, in the concrete?

In the book, *Connecting- the Mentoring Relationships You Need to Succeed in Life*, Paul Stanley relates this story: "On a recent flight I became engaged in a fascinating conversation with a psychologist who had a counseling practice to a wide social spectrum. As he related his concerns for the unprecedented rise in the number of people needing counseling, I detected compassion and frustration. He saw no solution to turn this trend around. At that point,

I suggested that there is a solution...reconciliation of man to God through Jesus Christ. He confessed that he came from a Christian home and church, but left them both as it appeared the gospel had little effect on those who embraced it. "I would say that more than two-thirds of my clients are practicing Christians!" he added. Then he said something profound. "Do you know the 'one-anothers' in the New Testament?" he questioned. I nodded, and he went on, "I am thoroughly convinced that if Christians practiced them to any degree at all, 90 percent of my Christian clients would not need me." Then he added, "And all the others—Christian or non-Christian— would flock to the church where it was happening."[6]

By my count there are about sixty "one-anothers" in the New Testament, verses that describe different ways we are to relate to one another. The presence of these directives is an explicit reminder that the Christian life isn't merely about "me and Jesus." It is about me and the Lord and his people, it is about the community we experience with the Father, Son and Holy Spirit and one another—the grand fellowship of the Kingdom.

Here is a sampling of the one-anothers:

"Be devoted to one another in love. Honor one another above yourselves." (Romans 12.10)

"Accept one another, then, just as Christ accepted you, in order to bring praise to God." (Romans 15.7)

"You, my brothers and sisters, were called to be free. But do not use your freedom to indulge the sinful nature; rather, serve one another humbly in love." (Galatians 5.13)

"Carry each other's burdens, and in this way you will fulfill the law of Christ." (Galatians 6.2)

---

6   Paul D. Stanley and J. Robert Clinton, *Connecting- The Mentoring Relationships You Need to Succeed in Life*, Carol Stream; Navpress, 1992, 175-76

"Be kind and compassionate to one another, forgiving each other, just as in Christ God forgave you." (Ephesians 4.32)

"Do nothing out of selfish ambition or vain conceit. Rather, in humility value others above yourselves." (Philippians 2.3)

"Let the message of Christ dwell among you richly as you teach and admonish one another with all wisdom..." (Colossians 3.16)

"Therefore encourage one another and build each other up, just as in fact you are doing." (1 Thessalonians 5.11)

"And let us consider how we may spur one another on toward love and good deeds." (Hebrews 10.24)

"Therefore confess your sins to each other and pray for each other so that you may be healed. The prayer of a righteous person is powerful and effective." (James 5.16)

"Offer hospitality to one another without grumbling. Each of you should use whatever gift you have received to serve others, as faithful stewards of God's grace in its various forms." (1 Peter 4.9-10)

Loving People Means Acting in Their Best Interests

Several of the one-anothers tell us simply to "love one another." It's my contention that all of the other passages expand on and make concrete what it means to love another person. Further, I believe that the one-anothers, taken together as a descriptive definition of active love, communicate the idea that loving people means acting in their best interests.

Let me repeat that: Loving people means acting in their best interests. Not their best comfort, not their preferences, but in their biblical, eternal best interests. The actions that meet the "best-interest" criterion are not always easy to determine, as the situation with my friend at the beginning of the chapter illustrates. Many Christian business people caught in the tensions of profit, company loyalty and love for individuals can also testify to the challenge of acting in someone's best interests. But this definition does add some clarity and concreteness to the culturally vague notion of love.

Again, to act in peoples' best interests is not the same as acting in keeping with their preferences. Some very sick people don't want to go to the hospital, but there are times when loving friends or relatives simply need to look them in the eyes and announce that they are being taken in right now. Other people are not comfortable with, and may even be hostile to, communication about Jesus Christ. They want nothing to do with Christianity. But if we love them we will still try to reach them, still try to bring the reality of Jesus Christ into their lives in relevant ways, in ways they can understand and relate to. There is a possibility that some who are reading this now were once at that point: You were obnoxiously anti-church or anti-Christ. But someone loved you enough to reach out to you according to your best interests, not your preferences or philosophical leanings at the time.

Over the years I've been part of several Toastmasters clubs that seek to develop people in the area of public speaking. First-timers are often surprised to discover that every aspect of the meeting is evaluated—from the opening greeting, to the announcements, to the chairmanship, to the prepared speeches. An unofficial slogan that comes up again and again is, "Whitewash is for the fence!" The point is that a phony, superficial evaluation that says an individual's performance was just fine—in essence a whitewash evaluation—has no place in the meeting. Evaluations are to be honest and actively help people improve. Yes, evaluations can hurt in some measure, but a good evaluation is an act of love and respect. It is in the best interest of the individual receiving the evaluation.

One of the most cutting passages in the New Testament is also one of the most poetic and sentimental. And it further clarifies this concrete active love to which Christ Followers are called:

> *"If I speak with human eloquence and angelic ecstasy*
> *but don't love, I'm nothing but the creaking of a rusty*
> *gate. If I speak God's Word with power, revealing*
> *all his mysteries and making everything plain as day,*
> *and if I have faith that says to a mountain, "Jump,"*
> *and it jumps, but I don't love, I'm nothing. If I give*
> *everything I own to the poor and even go to the*
> *stake to be burned as a martyr, but I don't love, I've*
> *gotten nowhere. So, no matter what I say, what I*
> *believe, and what I do, I'm bankrupt without love." (1*
> *Corinthians 13.1-3)[7]*

If you really want to squirm, insert your name in place of the pronouns: "If Daren speaks with human eloquence…Daren is bankrupt without love."

Now crank it up a notch. Move into verses 4-7:

> *"Love never gives up.*
> *Love cares more for others than for self.*
> *Love doesn't want what it doesn't have.*
> *Love doesn't strut,*
> *Doesn't have a swelled head,*
> *Doesn't force itself on others,*
> *Isn't always 'me first,'*
> *Doesn't fly off the handle,*
> *Doesn't keep score of the sins of others,*
> *Doesn't revel when others grovel,*
> *Takes pleasure in the flowering of truth,*
> *Puts up with anything,*

---

7   Scripture taken from THE MESSAGE, Copyright © 1993, 1994, 1995, 1996, 2000, 2001, 2002. Used by permission of NavPress Publishing Group

Trusts God always,
Always looks for the best,
Never looks back,
But keeps going to the end."
1 Corinthians 13.4-7[8]

Now insert your name in the place of "love." "Daren never gives up, Daren cares more for others than for himself…"

Loving People is Not Abstract

If you're anything like me, this exercise cuts through whatever façade of spirituality you are currently trying to hide behind, and reveals the truth of your heart's current love posture. It often exposes me as a fraud based on the way I've recently treated someone; other times, gratefully and by the grace of God, it encourages me when it highlights evidence of the life of Christ flowing through me. This passage takes the abstractness of love and moves it irresistibly to the concrete; it removes the temptation for me to say "I am loving" simply because I am feeling good about myself, despite how I am actually dealing with family, friends and strangers.

Many years ago I heard one of my preaching heroes, Haddon Robinson, speak on this passage at a denominational event. I can't imagine a more difficult passage to address before pastors, professors and church leadership—it's just too familiar. But Dr. Robinson, of course, nailed it. I've never forgotten his summary statement: "Love is that thing which if a church has it, doesn't really need much else, and if it doesn't have it, whatever else it does have doesn't really matter much." To capture the full impact of his summary, substitute your name for "church" and the related pronouns: "Love is that thing which if Daren has it, he doesn't really need much else, and if he doesn't have it, whatever else he does have doesn't really matter."

So much for hiding behind the supposed abstractness of love!

---

8 Ibid

Whenever I need a reminder of the practical side of love, I read this pledge from the classic book, *Love Acceptance and Forgiveness* by Jerry Cook:

> "'Brother, I want you to know that I'm committed to you. You'll never knowingly suffer at my hands. I'll never say or do anything, knowingly, to hurt you. I'll always in every circumstance seek to help you and support you. If you're down and I can lift you up, I'll do that. Anything I have that you need, I'll share with you; and if need be I'll give it to you. No matter what I find out about you and no matter what happens in the future, either good or bad, my commitment to you will never change. And there's nothing you can do about it. You don't have to respond. I love you and that's what it means.'"[9]

Can you imagine the security and joy of participating in a community marked by that kind of concrete love?

Back to the story of my faux-suicidal friend at the beginning of the chapter. Was I acting in love, in his best interests, when I told his wife to make the call to the police? I wasn't really sure at the time, but I have come to believe so. My thoughts in the heat of the moment were that he likely wasn't actually suicidal, but I didn't know for sure, and decided to act on his claims. Further, I reasoned, if he wasn't suicidal but simply playing head games with his wife, a run in with the authorities might be a much-needed "slap upside the head" to make him think twice about messing around in that way again. The fact that I'm still friends with this individual is a good indication that, despite his anger with me at the time, he realized that I do, in fact, care for him and want the best for him. (It's true and it always will be true, buddy!)

---

9   Jerry Cook, *Love Acceptance and Forgiveness*, Ventura: Regal Books, 1979, 13

Growing as a Lover of People

How are you doing as a lover of people? Are you living out the "one-anothers" at home, work, school, church? Does your name fit comfortably in the place of "love" in 1 Corinthians 13?

Here are some questions to spark your growth in becoming a lover of people:

1. Are you acting in the best interests of the key people in your life? Think about immediate family, coworkers, neighbors, classmates.

1. How are you doing with the following, especially challenging one-anothers: forgiving, admonishing, accepting? Have you learned how to love people even when they disagree with you, and you them?

1. Who do you need to love this week by helping them in a practical way through physical help, financial help or by giving them your undivided attention for a significant period of time?

To be a lover of people means to do all these things, and more. Not because all the people we will be called to greet, encourage, challenge, help or forgive are warm and cuddly, but because they have an inherent eternal value and because they are loved by the God we claim to love and serve.

A Christ Follower is a lover of people, someone who acts in the best interests of others because they see the inherent value in all people, and because they love the God who loves everyone.

CHAPTER 5

Holy

*(Jesus Christ) "...who gave himself for us to redeem
us from all wickedness, and to purify for himself a
people that are his very own, eager to do what is good."*
(Titus 2.14)

The largest body of contaminated water in the United States is the Berkeley Pit located in Butte, Montana. The pit is an old mine site surrounded by more than 3500 miles of tunnels and other mine workings that started in 1865. When the pumps that kept the mines free of water were turned off, water levels rose and washed arsenic and lead and other toxins into the pit, which now contains about 30 billion gallons of poison, and so much dissolved copper that it can actually be mined from the water. Several years ago, more than 300 snow geese landed in the pit to rest during their migration and all perished. But the situation could get worse. When the water level in the pit reaches the height of the water table, perhaps within a decade, the toxic mix from the pit could seep into the ground water, polluting the surrounding water systems. To visit the old mine site and simply stand beside the water, you are required to take a certified hazardous materials course.

Interestingly, life has been discovered in the Berkeley Pit. It started when a researcher noticed a clump of algae floating on the surface. Further research has led to the discovery of 160 different life forms thriving in the toxic lake. These organisms—among a group called extremophiles because of their ability to live in conditions that would kill most living things—have the ability to extract what they can use from the water and protect themselves from what is harmful. They actually clean up the water that surrounds them, creating a spot of health in the midst of the deadness. Some of these organisms are able to repair their own DNA when it gets damaged, which has led to speculation that there may be some medical discoveries arising from the mess.

Followers of Jesus Christ could be described as extremophiles. We are called to live in, thrive in, and transform a culture that is often opposed to God. This is not to say that our entire culture is poisonous—it's not. Nor should we withdraw from culture for our own safety. The call to be salt and light requires we remain engaged.

But how to do that—to actually live as worshippers of the one true God, as followers of the Lord Jesus in a world largely opposed to him—has been a challenge for God's people from before the time of Christ.

We've seen that a Christ Follower is first of all a lover of God and secondly a lover of people. Some might declare that these are not just the top two, but the only two nonnegotiable character traits. However, this third quality, alluded to in the Berkeley Pit story, is just as integral to the life of a Christ Follower.

There is a word, which, along with its derivatives shows up more than 600 times in the Bible. The word means, in part, to be different. And that word is "holy".

> (God) "...who has saved us and called us to a holy life—not because of anything we have done but because of his own purpose and grace." (2 Timothy 1.9)
>
> "And by that will, we have been made holy through the sacrifice of the body of Jesus Christ once for all." (Hebrews 10.10)

"As obedient children, do not conform to the evil desires you had when you lived in ignorance. But just as he who called you is holy, so be holy in all you do; for it is written: 'Be holy, because I am holy.'" (1 Peter 1.14-16)

In addition to being a lover of God and a lover of people, a Christ Follower is holy. This means, in part, to be different, in a good way. There are some Christ Followers who are "different," but not necessarily holy. I think of the wide assortment of quirky individuals I've known through the years. In some cases they indeed may have been believers, but they ranged from the immoral to the obnoxious to the plain old weird. A church friend of mine worked in a saw mill with one such believer. The person commented one day how much he was being persecuted for his faith on the jobsite. My friend took him aside and explained to him that he wasn't being persecuted because he was a Christian, he was being persecuted because he was a jerk. Holiness is not merely being "different," it is about distinctiveness in moral character and action.

God is holy. He is entirely separate from his creation. He is awesome and majestic. He is totally morally pure. There is no evil or wrong in him. A core meaning of the word holy is to be "set apart." So to say a Christ Follower is holy and called to be holy is to say that a follower of Jesus is morally different and in some way set apart for different purposes than those who are not following the Lord. Throughout the New Testament there is an emphasis on both the ethical aspect of holiness (conduct) as well as the inner aspect of holiness (character).

Reasons for Holiness

Why would a person want to live a holy life, a different life, a set-apart life? What would be the purpose or motivation for doing so?

Personally, I have seen in my own life a direct relationship between my practical holiness and my effectiveness as a pastor, husband and parent. I have seen a direct relationship between my holiness and my level of joy, peace and contentment. When I am walking in the Holy Spirit, walking in holiness, I am truly at my best in every way.

Not surprisingly, I have also seen a direct relationship between my holiness and my effectiveness in evangelism. Thinking back to some unholy phases of my life, it is possible that there are some people in hell right now due, in part, to my lack of holiness. The way I was living made it impossible for me to share Christ. My life was a testimony against him. By God's grace there are others who have come to Christ because they came into my life at a time when I was on track with God, when I was living out my set-apartness.

Why live a holy life? Here are a few good reasons:

1. To please God, as a way of showing gratitude. God calls us to be holy and he loved us and gave himself for us. Living a holy life is a grateful, God-honouring response to what he has done. I think of the DeGarmo and Key song *The Pledge* from my younger years which contains the lyrics *"He died for me, I'll live for him."*

2. Holy lives change lives. Lives that are set apart for God are used by God to reach others. Christians and churches that just blend in and are different in no way from the general culture challenge no one and change nothing. I once saw some data that was summarized this way: The more closely aligned a church is with its culture, the more quickly that church will decline. If all we do is reflect our culture, if we mindlessly endorse everything about it, we are no longer salt and light, we are no longer different. And salt that loses its saltiness "is no longer good for anything…" Holy lives change lives, holy churches change communities, in part because they call people to something different and greater.

3. Holiness and spiritual power go hand in hand. The more you and I live out the reality that we are set apart by God, the greater our spiritual power to be his agent on this earth. Being filled with and led by the Holy Spirit, the Spirit of Power, is part of what it means and what it takes to live a holy life.

The Old Testament book of Judges tells the story of Samson. His parents vowed, among other things, that his hair wouldn't be cut. It was a symbol of his set apartness, his holiness in God's eyes. And even when Samson did some unholy things, God honored that promise of set apartness. But one day Delilah got to him, and he shared his secret:

> "So he told her everything. 'No razor has ever been used on my head,' he said, 'because I have been a Nazirite dedicated to God from my mother's womb. If my head were shaved, my strength would leave me, and I would become as weak as any other man.'"
> (Judges 16.17)

"As weak as any other man." And indeed, the story reveals that he was now as weak as any other man, and the terrible consequences he paid for forsaking his set-apartness.

Unholy (in conduct) Christians, who are not living out their set-apartness are spiritually weak. They can't overcome temptation, they can't effectively share Christ, they can't engage victoriously in spiritual warfare, nor can they be the hands and feet and mouth of Jesus Christ, as they are called to be. If you want spiritual power, if you want to do something significant for the cause of Christ, for eternity, a holy life is a given, it's an absolute prerequisite.

Holiness is a relevant issue because heaven and hell and eternity are relevant issues. As Maximus, the main character in the movie Gladiator says, "What we do in this life echoes throughout eternity". Holiness or unholiness on the part of God's people rumbles through eternity. For some people around us, our holiness or unholiness is an issue of life or death. So let's not fool ourselves into thinking this topic is churchy and ethereal and irrelevant. It's not!

Holiness is More Than Do's and Don'ts

One of the problems we have with this issue of holiness is that we immediately think of the do's and don'ts—the actions that are holy and unholy. This is not without merit; the New Testament frequently highlights the outer, behavioural aspects of holiness. For example:

- *"Do not judge or you too will be judged"* (Matthew 7.1)
- *"Love each other as I have loved you"* (John 15.12)
- *"Do not take revenge..."* (Romans 12.19)
- *"...put off falsehood and speak truthfully..."* (Ephesians 4.25)
- *"...get rid of moral filth and the evil that is so prevalent..."* (James 1.21)

But what we do is only one aspect of holiness. And unless we understand another aspect of holiness, we will wallow in defeat in the area of our conduct.

> *"I'm weary of sinning and stumbling, repenting and falling again;*
> *I'm tired of resolving and striving, and finding the struggle so vain.*
> *I long for an arm to uphold me, a will that is stronger than mine;*
> *A Saviour to cleanse me and fill me, and keep me by power divine."*

Those words from A.B. Simpson's hymn, *I Want to Be Holy*, echo the heart cry of many Christ Followers. Have you ever been there? Are you there now? How do we move on from this place?

At the start of many of the letters to the churches in the New Testament, the people of the church are referred to as holy, in some translations they are called "saints" which means holy ones. For instance, the greeting to the church in Ephesus goes this way: *"Paul, an apostle of Christ Jesus by the will of God, to God's holy people in Ephesus, the faithful in Christ Jesus."* (Ephesians 1.1)

Those Ephesian people were a good bunch, for a while anyway. I can understand Paul calling them God's holy people. Some translations simply describe them as "saints" which means holy ones. But what about the rowdies who made up the church at Corinth? Paul referred to them in that letter as immature babies—they bickered and fought all the time. Sexual immorality was prevalent in the church. Some of them got drunk at their common meals. And yet the letter starts this way: *"To the church of God in Corinth, to those sanctified in Christ Jesus and called to be his holy people..."* (1 Corinthians 1.2)

How is it that this bunch of unholy (in conduct) people are described as "sanctified" (set apart, made holy) in Christ Jesus? Was Paul just being polite before he rebuked them for their very unholy conduct? Not at all. He was referring to the fact that people in the Corinthian church were holy not because they were noticeably different than the world around them. They were holy because they were chosen by God, and declared holy by God, based on the sacrifice of Christ, and indwelt by the Holy Spirit. They were "sanctified in Christ Jesus" —that was their spiritual location or position and their true identity. Additionally, they were called to be holy—the striving of his Spirit and the witness of the Word of God was drawing them, calling them to an actual practice of holiness, a holy life. The NASB version describes them as "saints by calling" perhaps subtly communicating that there is a gap between who they presently are and who they are called to be.

Perhaps this, or some variation, happened to you: You were going through life and came to understand that something was not quite right. You came to appreciate that there is a God who created you and who had moral standards that you had broached repeatedly. In biblical terms, you came to understand that *"all (including you) have sinned and fall short of the glory of God."* (Romans 3.23)

Eventually, you also realized, *"the wages of sin is death but the gift of God is eternal life in Jesus Christ our Lord."* (Romans 6.23) You somehow—through reading the Word or through the witness of a friend—came to realize that Jesus Christ came and died to pay the price for all those sins. The Spirit did a work with that truth in your heart and mind, and you repented and trusted in Jesus for forgiveness. At that moment, at that instant, totally apart from any visible difference in you, God declared you holy—he declared you his, he set you apart for himself. Your sin was removed and the perfection of Jesus Christ was applied to you. You didn't deserve it. You didn't earn it. It was purely an act of God in response to your faith in the sacrifice of Jesus Christ. When we receive Jesus Christ as our Saviour, God sets us apart to and for himself. We are, as in 1 Corinthians, "sanctified in Christ Jesus."

That is why the worldly, immoral Christians in Corinth were described as sanctified: They were holy on the basis of being in a faith relationship with God through Jesus Christ. In other words, every Christian is holy, every Christian is a saint. Why? Because every Christian has been chosen by God and declared holy by him based on a faith that accesses the benefits of the sacrifice of Jesus. It has nothing to do with our practical perfection. It has to do with Christ's perfection being applied to us. This can be difficult to wrap our brains around, but it is a foundational truth we must embrace if we are to move ahead into practical holiness. The truth is, if you have repented of your sins and put your faith in Jesus Christ, you are holy by the declaration of God, totally apart from how holy your behaviour or thinking is right now. You are his. At the core, our holiness, like our basic forgiveness, is about God's gift, not our effort.

Most children and probably most adults have junk they just won't get rid of. I've got a little piece of diamond willow, a few belt buckles, some rusty fish hooks I found snorkelling when I was a teenager and other assorted trinkets that I have kept since the day I got them. I'm sure you are the same. You have junk that's not worth much of anything from a purely material standpoint. But it's special. And it's yours. And despite the questions raised by family and friends, perhaps your spouse, you refuse to part with your treasures!

In the same way, someone may look at you, and you may even look at yourself, thinking "I'm not special. I'm a poor, weak Christ Follower. I'm not worth much from an eternal perspective." But God says, "No! You're mine and I'm keeping you!" Let that truth soak in for a moment. Totally apart from your current level of "victory" or actual holy conduct, if you have repented and put your faith in Jesus Christ, God looks at you and says, "You are mine, and I love you. I treasure you, and I'm keeping you!"

I need to hear that often. Probably you do, too. So know it, hear it. If you have repented of your sins and put your faith in Jesus, God has chosen you, he calls you holy, he calls you his. It is impossible to function in a truly holy manner, to exhibit practical holiness, until we are secure in this positional holiness that rests in an act of God.

Holiness Becomes Visible

I entered into that positional aspect of holiness as a child in elementary school when I understood that Jesus had died for me and I needed forgiveness. I accepted him as my Saviour. But there was little in my life in terms of practical holiness until I was about 20 years old. I was at a stage in life where I was doing everything I wanted to do. On one level, life was perfect. Yet for some reason I was miserable. Over time I came to understand that it had something to do with my relationship with God.

I claimed to believe in Jesus Christ, and in fact did, but there was little visible evidence. After a lengthy, miserable inner battle that often surfaced with tears of frustration and emptiness when I was alone, I came to the place where I got out of the driver's seat and Jesus got into it. Some people refer to this as "making him Lord of my life" or yielding fully to him or surrendering to him. We might dispute the accuracy of some of the phrases used, but the intent is to express a change in relationship.

This event is not unrelated to being filled with the Holy Spirit, and often it is associated with believer baptism. A person who came to Christ years ago finally decides to be fully obedient, and as a part of that new life of obedience chooses to be baptized. In my life, the change I experienced at the age of 20 was more dramatic, more emotionally intense, and led to more significant life change than when I had first come to faith in Christ. My conduct and overall spiritual life stabilized, and while perfection didn't suddenly appear, there was immediate and ongoing growth and progress. As I have talked with and counselled others, it seems that my experience is not unusual, especially among those raised in the evangelical church world.

Is there any biblical precedent for this sort of thing or is it a modern day, western, evangelical aberration?

The book of Romans has eleven chapters of deep, solid doctrine, explaining how God has worked and is working in history to bring people—first the Jews and ultimately people from all nations—into a right relationship with himself. We were created for relationship with him. Then in the next chapter, after the doctrinal foundation is thoroughly laid, we read:

> *"Therefore, I urge you, brothers and sisters, in view of God's mercy, to offer your bodies as a living sacrifice, holy and pleasing to God—this is true worship. Do not conform to the pattern of this world, but be transformed by the renewing of your mind." (Romans 12.1-2)*

Note that this is addressed to believers, to people who, like the Ephesians and Corinthians, are *"loved by God and called to be his holy people"* (Romans 1.7) The call of Romans 12 is for a conscious alignment of our conduct with how God sees us and what he is calling us to. In a sense it's an endorsement of the fact that we are set apart and agree with that set-apartness. It's like the lights go on and we say, "Huh, God has set me apart, I am holy, I am his. I need to set myself apart for him and his purposes." It is at this point that we align ourselves with God's declaration of our positional holiness and his call for our practical holiness. When we arrive at this place, with the indwelling Holy Spirit now also filling and controlling us, our conduct begins to reflect our calling.

Shouldn't this happen when you accept and begin following Jesus? Yes, it probably should. But before we are too hard on "modern Christians" please note that the sense of the imperative in Romans 12.2 indicates that they should "quit conforming to the world..." That's right—these early New Testament followers of Jesus Christ needed to be explicitly told to quit conforming to the values of the world that were contrary to the character and calling of Christ.

Why doesn't it click in for us sooner? Is this not part of what it means to repent when we initially respond to the Gospel?

The answers will vary with the individual, and it seems that those who come to Christ later in life, or have a more intense conversion experience, are more likely to offer themselves fully to God from the start of their following of Jesus, even as they are receiving his forgiveness. For people like me, raised in a church, when you come to Christ for salvation you are often coming primarily for forgiveness to get into heaven. "Fire insurance" some call it. At that point of receiving basic forgiveness (often at a young age), you may not understand the full implications of the Christian life, especially the ultimate goal of Christlikeness. You may not be aware that you are called to be holy. But over time, perhaps quite quickly if you are immersed in scripture or in a good mentoring relationship, you understand God's claim on you because of what Jesus did. *"In view of God's mercy..."* as it says in Romans 12.1 you realize you are called to respond. At this point, a struggle often begins: Who will be the boss—me or God? Am I going to set myself apart as he has set me apart, am I going to endorse this call on my life that I am just now realizing is part of following Jesus?

The alternative to offering ourselves is that we will be discontented, even miserable, with our state. This discontent is the mercy of God, the conviction of the Holy Spirit. He will allow us to have no real rest until we offer ourselves completely to him. Why? Because God's plan is not just to forgive us, not just to get us into heaven, but to make us like Jesus, in character. And part of that is to make us holy in our actual conduct.

How does that happen? Assuming we are truly followers of Jesus Christ—we have repented of our sins and put our faith in him for salvation—and we understand that God has set us apart and we desire to grow in practical holiness, in holy conduct, what do we do?

Growing in Holiness

If we try to live like a Christ Follower when we haven't fully yielded to him, as in Romans 12.1-2, it will be an exercise in futility and possibly a path to legalism where we make up rules to keep rather than being ruled by God.

I used to own and enjoy a sailboard. One of the lakes I frequented had some very good sailboarders with high-end equipment. The lake was a bit of a wind tunnel and frequently offered ideal conditions for sailboarding. Some of these high-level sailboarders would head out in wind and water that would keep me and the other light-weights on the shore. But there were times when even the really good sailboarders with the very best equipment couldn't go out. And it wasn't when the wind got really wild. It was when the wind died right down. At that point it didn't matter how skilled they were or how good their equipment was. When there was no wind, there was no sailboarding.

And so it is with growth in holiness. You can work at trying to imitate Christlike character and conduct all you want, following whatever "holiness checklist" is used in your particular group. But unless you offer yourself to God and move into the fullness of the Holy Spirit, the place where he is in charge and you aren't, very little character growth will occur. The good news is that the moment we are ready to give up control he is ready to take over. But we need to understand that we need him. Growth in holiness is like a joint venture between the individual and God—your part is to offer yourself to him while his part is to fill you, empower you and change you.

Scripture indicates that the Holy Spirit is resident in everyone who has come into a right relationship with God through Jesus Christ:

"And if anyone does not have the Spirit of Christ, they
do not belong to Christ." (Romans 8.9)
"Do you know that your bodies are temples of the Holy
Spirit, who is in you, whom you have received from
God?" (1 Corinthians 6.19)

Scripture also indicates the need for followers of Jesus Christ to be continually or repeatedly filled with the Holy Spirit, which is the intent of the command in Ephesians 5.18 where we are called not to be drunk with wine but filled with (controlled by) the Holy Spirit. The alternative to being controlled by the Holy Spirit is being controlled by our short-term pleasure seeking sin nature. So, we are either living in alignment with our sin nature, holy in position but not practice, or we are living as Spirit controlled Christ Followers, holy both in our position and our conduct.

"So I say, walk by the Spirit, and you will not gratify
the desires of the sinful nature." (Galatians 5.16)

The issue of temptation is relevant at this point, for it is temptation that leads us to live outside of our calling to be holy in both position and practice. The presence of temptation is not an indication of a lower level of holiness or Christlikeness. Jesus was tempted, intensely—yet he never sinned.

For us to experience ongoing progress in practical, ethical holiness, it is helpful to identify any patterns of temptation and sin and take steps to overcome or break those patterns. Recognition of such patterns usually comes through the interface of the Spirit of God and the Word of God in our hearts and minds. Overcoming those patterns once they surface takes place through the power of the Word, the indwelling Holy Spirit and often the community of Christ. It is very difficult, and by God's design sometimes impossible, to break deep seated sin patterns apart from the encouragement, prayer, accountability and support of fellow Christ Followers. Though we might refer to holiness as "personal holiness," due to the nature of the Body of Christ, it is never only about us. We were not made to follow Jesus alone, we do it together.

A promise I continually come back to when it seems my progress in practical holiness has stalled out or taken a backward track is this one:

> "May God himself, the God of peace, sanctify you through and through. May your whole spirit, soul and body be kept blameless at the coming of our Lord Jesus Christ. The one who calls you is faithful, and he will do it." (1 Thessalonians 5.23-24)

Amen.

It is God's desire and his call to us that we be holy on the inside and on the outside, in position and practice, in every corner of our personality, in every facet of our being. The one who calls us is faithful, and he will do it.

————•—•—————

A Christ Follower is both holy and growing in holiness, endorsing God's declaration of their holiness by setting themselves apart for him, and drawing on the power of the indwelling Holy Spirit to live in a way that reflects their identity as saints.

————•—•—————

CHAPTER 6

Truth-Based

"All scripture is God-breathed and is useful...."
2 *Timothy 3.16*

"This book has really helped me," the sharply dressed woman said. "Can you read it and tell me what you think?"

"Absolutely!" I said. I had previously given her a small gospel pamphlet to read and didn't want to appear closed-minded.

The author of the book was a high-profile psychic who taught on reincarnation, astral projection and communication with the dead. I read it carefully, though only when I was fully awake and with prayer for protection before and after. Each chapter had meditation exercises which I chose not to do as they were in blatant opposition to the teaching of scripture. Then I faced the difficult task of providing feedback. I settled on a small card with a brief note inserted:

Dear _____,

Thanks for the privilege of hearing some of your story and for the loan of your book. I thought there were some good nuggets on grief, forgiveness and relationships.

I have some concerns with the whole spirit guide thing and talking to the dead, based on the Bible as well as my own dealings with the spirit world. I believe, and have seen firsthand evidence, that demons are real and will do anything to deceive people. And one of their basic strategies is to pretend they are good.

Another issue is obviously reincarnation. The Bible teaches that we are appointed to die once and after that face judgment and eternity—no reruns!

Perhaps what bothered me most were her references to Jesus Christ who taught resurrection not reincarnation. He said, "I am the way and the truth and the life, no one comes to the Father except through me." This doesn't mean that he is right or that what I believe is right, but simply that Jesus and the author of your book can't both be right—they are teaching two completely different things. So we need to make sure we have good reasons to believe whoever we choose to believe. For me, I see pretty good evidence for the fact that Jesus was resurrected, as he predicted, and that helps me accept his authority on other matters.

I love to kick this stuff around, it's not just part of my job, it's my passion! If you ever want to talk more, have any questions about that little booklet I gave you or have other authors you can suggest I read, please feel free to call.

All the best in your year ahead,

Daren

Given the many different varieties of spiritual teaching, much of it contradicting or incompatible with other teachings, on what basis can a person accept and believe one brand of spirituality and reject another? Is it arrogant to believe that one way of thinking is right and another is wrong? What place does absolute truth hold for the Christ Follower?

So far we've seen that a Christ Follower is a Lover of God, a Lover of People and Holy. There are many scriptures that talk about the fourth character quality. Here is a sampling:

> *"Do your best to present yourself to God as one approved, a worker who does not need to be ashamed and who correctly handles the word of truth." (2 Timothy 2.15)*

"For the time will come when people will not put up with sound doctrine. Instead, to suit their own desires, they will gather around them a great number of teachers to say what their itching ears want to hear. They will turn their ears away from the truth and turn aside to myths." (2 Timothy 4.3-4.)

"Stand firm then, with the belt of truth buckled around your waist..." (Ephesians 6.14)

The fourth character quality: A Christ Follower is truth-based.

What's the opposite of being truth-based, having your worldview and philosophical foundation established on truth? At best it is to be opinion-based; at worst, lie-based, built on falsehood.

One of my favorite stories about lying was reported in MacLean's magazine:

"After stopping for a few drinks at a bar, a Zimbabwean bus driver found that the 20 mental patients he was supposed to be transporting had escaped. Not wanted to admit his incompetence, the driver went to a nearby bus stop and offered people in line a free ride. He then delivered the passengers to the mental hospital, telling staff that the patients were very excitable and prone to bizarre fantasies. The deception wasn't discovered for three days."[10]

Funny...but there are likely some less than funny stories that could be told by some of the passengers who became patients!

A Christ Follower, a disciple of Jesus, is truth-based. This assumes, of course, that God has given us a source of absolute truth, a reference point in a world of competing options and opinions. The idea that there is such a reference point is disputed by many today, and not just by those who hold to a materialistic worldview. There is now a wide spectrum of spirituality that encourages people to trust

---

10 *Maclean's*, Dec 13, 1999, page 14

their feelings, personal experiences and intuitions, and to reject their teachers, books, and even words.

Since the majority of those who read this book will come from the perspective of accepting the Bible as trustworthy and true, the Word of God, and since there are many other books that thoroughly and ably deal with the arguments surrounding that conclusion, this chapter is primarily an explanation of what it means to be truth-based rather than an argument for the truthfulness and trustworthiness of the Bible.

If, for some reason, you do not currently accept the Bible as God's Word, here's an interesting question for you to wrestle with: "What is your reference point, what is your source of truth?"

It's easy to say, "I don't believe the Bible. I don't believe God has communicated in a clear and relevant way." It is a lot tougher to follow it up with an explanation of what you do believe and why. It's also easy to say, "There is no such thing as 'truth!'" But no one has yet figured out how to consistently live out the implications of that idea. And no one who makes this argument seems willing to jump off a high roof and disprove the law or "truth" of gravity.

In my observation, it seems that many people simply put their faith in someone else's opinions with no real reflection on the consequences of relying on the wrong source of truth. I had a friend some years ago who, when I shared biblical concepts with him, brushed me off with "The Bible's not true— it's been proven!" and I would simply reply, "Okay then, prove it to me. Show me these proofs." But he never did—he was simply piggy-backing on someone else's opinions without having wrestled through the issues himself.

When I was in grade 6, my friends and I learned how to make match guns from clothes pins. When you pulled the trigger, a "strike anywhere" match was lit and fired ten or fifteen feet. One day at lunch break three of us were firing matches into the thick matted grass behind the school, letting it burn for a while and then putting it out. At one point my friend Mark shot a match into the grass and the other two of us jokingly held him back so he couldn't put it out right away. The fire quickly grew to a large circle of burning grass.

When we finally let him go, it was too big for all of us to stamp out. So we did what any normal grade six boys would do—we bolted. Several kids from our school saw us as we ran from the billowing smoke.

Before I got to my house three blocks away I heard the sirens of fire trucks. I walked in the door and immediately said to my father, who was a police officer, "Someone started a fire at the school and people are trying to blame me." Lunch break wasn't even over and the police were at my door to question me. My father, taking my word for it, said to his coworkers, "You've got the wrong guy—it was someone else." The police then tracked down my accomplices who, of course, implicated me. When the truth surfaced it was not a happy day.

Many people live their lives in that same way, manufacturing lies that they treat as truth so they can live the way they want without consequences. It's fun for a time, but then one day the real truth surfaces—the lies are exposed and the consequences show up.

A Christ Follower is truth-based, which means primarily "Bible-based". This does not mean that the Bible contains all truth. People who accept the authority of the Bible sometimes react negatively to that statement. But the point is that all of the possible truth in the universe is not contained in the Bible. For instance, the Bible says very little about hunting and absolutely nothing about hockey. (If it did, I might be better at both!) But while the Bible doesn't contain all truth, all that it contains is truth. And the truths it contains are the most important ones, for they relate to the big issues of life and death and eternity. Additionally, even if a topic or situation is not specifically addressed in the Bible, there are principles that can be applied and give direction.

So, to be truth-based means that your beliefs and actions are founded on the Bible. The obvious questions that arise are:

1. What does that mean? And more importantly,

2. Am I truth-based?

Don't answer the second question too quickly—certainly not before you have answered the first. Be bold enough to take an honest look at yourself and ask questions such as

Am I really truth-based?

- Is my church and my small group truth-based?
- Are the books, even the Christian books, I'm allowing to shape my life really based on the Bible—or are they simply someone's opinions?
- Does a commitment to truth show up not just in my formal or informal personal statement of belief, or my church's statement of faith, but also in the way my life is lived and the way the church and ministries I support operate?
- Is the Bible demonstrably my foundation of truth, my "rule of faith and practice" as so many doctrinal statements say, or have I simply adopted the concept of being "Bible-based" without allowing it to permeate my life?

Let's provide some more fodder with which to answer those questions. As I have come to understand it, being truth-based, Bible-based, includes three components.

Component #1: Know the Bible

When I was fourteen, I signed up to read the Bible through in a year. For the first several months I stayed on schedule, dropped off a bit through the summer, picked up a bit in the fall, and then in the last week of the year, between Christmas and New Year's Day, I read for hours every day to get it done—which I did.

That exercise changed me. Simply spending so much time in the Word is bound to chip away at anyone's soul, and it did mine. Even though I'd been in Sunday School and church from the time of conception, reading the Bible through gave me a massive infusion of raw truth. I gained a big-picture look at God's work in history. Among other things, I asked to be baptized because I saw how it wasn't merely a command, but also an assumption for followers of Jesus. Additionally, I was taken by the incredible unity of the Book, despite being composed of so many smaller books by so many authors over so many centuries. From a young age I'd been a reader, often reading for hours every day and long into the night—reading books that were written for much older audiences. But I'd never read anything like this. I couldn't have articulated it then, but I knew it was inspired, that God was behind it. A few years later when I again dove into the Word with a commitment not to read it through in a year, but to read it daily, it again began to do its work in me and led me first to a place of "total surrender," and ultimately to go to Bible college for a year "to get my head straight" and to learn to share my faith. I stayed for four years and ended up becoming a pastor.

Being truth-based means first of all that you know the Bible. This means to read it. Refer to it. Allow it to challenge, encourage, direct and teach you as needed. Go to it as a reference point for ideas and messages you are exposed to.

> *"Now the Berean Jews were of more noble character than those in Thessalonica, for they received the message with great eagerness and examined the Scriptures every day to see if what Paul said was true." (Acts 17.11)*

I can't tell you how many Christian leaders, myself included, wish our people were more Berean-like rather than being swayed by every wind of doctrine, every new idea that comes floating through Christian book stores, church websites and television programs. When you know the Bible you access it and draw on it again and again. It has a central place in your life.

Most churches have classes that help people get rooted in the Bible. A good church will be shaped by the proclamation of biblical truth, even if it is seeker-sensitive or seeker-driven in philosophy. In fact, in my observation, many seeker-driven churches are more shaped by biblical truth than some more traditional ones, and many mainline churches have more scripture read in their services than the nearby evangelical churches. In addition to the high-profile scripture will be given in a good church, there are many solid books and studies available to help individuals grow in their knowledge of the Word. But nothing beats picking up the Book itself and reading it under the direction of the Holy Spirit.

Many people find it helpful to use a Bible reading plan from time to time, and to read the Bible through in a year as I did at the age of fourteen. Different one-year reading plans are available online. There are even Bibles designed and laid out to help a person read them in a year. If you have never read the Bible from cover to cover, consider it for the year ahead. There is no need to wait for January 1st. You can start anytime. Reading the Bible helps you to know it, which is the foundation of being truth-based.

To know the Bible also means to memorize it. But why memorize it when you can simply read it, when you can have it at your fingertips on your phone? Scripture itself highlights the value of memorization:

> "I have hidden your word in my heart that I might not
> sin against you." (Psalm 119.11)

Jesus famously used memorized scripture to deal with temptation and fend off Satan in the wilderness, preceding his replies with the powerful words "It is written..."

The benefit of having God's truth in your heart and mind through your days and years cannot be overstated. It gives the Holy Spirit something to work with in your relationships and decision making, through your joys and challenges.

In the book, *The Church in China: How it Survives and Prospers Under Communism* there is a powerful report on the importance of internalizing scripture from a person who had been imprisoned:

> "We would pray, sing to ourselves, and write sermons in our
> minds to keep our minds clear. Those who did not know
> Scripture had a very bad time. Those who could not repeat
> scripture back to the Lord often either betrayed the master and

us, went insane, and/or committed suicide. It was the Word of God that kept us from doing any of the three."[11]

One Sunday during our college and seminary years, following a worship service at the church we attended, my wife Kristin and I were visiting with several people. A little girl named Catherine, about four years old, came up and said "I have a present for you from my heart." She then quoted from Psalm 100:

> *"Shout for joy to the Lord, all the earth. Worship the Lord with gladness; come before him with joyful songs."*
> *(Psalm 100.1-2)*

People ooed and aahed, some applauded and complimented her. But she interrupted and said, "I'm not done!" She then continued through the entire Psalm:

> *"Know that the Lord is God. It is he who made us, and we are his; we are his people, the sheep of his pasture. Enter his gates with thanksgiving and his courts with praise; give thanks to him and praise his name. For the Lord is good and his love endures forever; his faithfulness continues through all generations."*
> *(Psalm 100.3-5)*

We were impressed...and stunned. As my wife said later, "That little girl knows more scripture in one piece than I do!" A while later, Catherine's mother recited the book of James in an evening church service. We got to know Catherine's parents and learned that Catherine's mother Marilyn had not seemed very sharp as a young child. Her father prayed over her asking the Lord to heal her mind so that she could hide the Word in her heart. His prayer was answered and she was able to recite large portions of the Bible. In fact, as she described it to us, she didn't so much set out to memorize

---

11 Carl Lawrence, *The Church in China*. Minneapolis: Bethany House Publishers, 1985, 121

the passages, she just studied them so thoroughly that when she was done she knew them. More importantly, she was able to integrate them into her life and character. This lady became one of the most significant mentors my wife has ever had, even though they were only in the same community for two years.

With the motivation that came from our interaction with that little girl and her family, my wife began memorizing scripture by the chapter and book: James, Ephesians and assorted Psalms. I began with Matthew 5-7, the Sermon on the Mount. Then I decided that since I was planning to be a pastor I should learn the Pastoral letters: 1 & 2 Timothy and Titus. Later on, as a pastor preparing for ordination, I realized that the book of Romans addressed many major areas of doctrine, so I learned Romans. My wife has since learned several more of the letters, and chunks of the gospels and Psalms. I've added 1 Peter, Colossians, the first several chapters of Proverbs and a chunk of 1 Corinthians. Please understand, we are not brilliant people. We do not have photographic memories. In fact, I am a bit absent minded. It simply came down to making a decision to learn scripture.

Now, if you were to bump into me on the street and ask me to recite Romans or 1 Peter, could I do it flawlessly? Not likely—unless I'd recently reviewed it. But with prompting I could probably get it mostly right at any given time. My wife, who is far more rigorous with her reviewing than I am could come very close to perfection in reciting any passage she has learned at any time. But the point is not so much to be able to recite a passage on demand as to allow a passage to percolate through our hearts and souls and change our thinking, and to have it available to the Holy Spirit to lead and direct us in our decision-making. The directives to meditate on God's word seem to imply that we have immersed ourselves in it and are both reading and memorizing it.

Here is a pattern we have found helpful: Once a passage has been selected, break it into bite sized chunks, usually one or two chapters. Memorize the first verse or two. The next day review what you know and then carry on for a few more verses. Do this day after day until you have the section down. At that point you begin the review process. Go over the chapter or section every day for thirty days, then every week for ten weeks and after that every month for a year. Finally, every year go back over passages you have learned in the past. It might take a few days to get the kinks worked out of an old passage, but you will be surprised by how much you remember. The real benefit comes from the sheer volume of truth that the Holy Spirit has to work with to direct you, challenge you and bring to mind as you speak into the lives of others. In addition, if you teach the Bible, there is a depth that comes from being saturated in significant portions of the book.

Component #2: Believe the Bible

Many times—not all the time, but often—the people who make an effort to know the Book have already moved to the second part of being truth-based: they believe it. People who are truth-based know the Bible, and they also believe the Bible. They accept that it is God's Word, that it is absolute truth.

I've often had opportunity to explain to people why I believe the Bible. As I told my friend who gave me the book by the psychic, it really comes down to the person of Jesus Christ, and the credibility of Jesus comes down to the resurrection.

If Jesus did indeed rise from the dead, he has credibility—he can be trusted—and his opinion about scripture is worth considering. For starters, Jesus endorsed the Old Testament which was in existence in his day:

> "Do not think that I have come to abolish the Law or the Prophets; I have not come to abolish them but to fulfill them. Truly I tell you, until heaven and earth disappear, not the smallest letter, not the least stroke of a pen, will by any means disappear from the Law until everything is accomplished." (Matthew 5.17-18)

He also endorsed his key leaders, the apostles, and indicated that they would be the ones to transmit his story:

> *"But the Advocate, the Holy Spirit, whom the Father will send in my name, will teach you all things and will remind you of everything I have said to you."* (John 14.26)

> *"But when he, the Spirit of truth comes, he will guide you into all truth."* (John 16.13)

> *"But you will receive power when the Holy Spirit comes on you; and you will be my witnesses in Jerusalem, and in all Judea and Samaria, and to the ends of the earth."* (Acts 1.8)

We even have Peter describing the writings of Paul as scripture in 1 Peter 3.15-16.

But it all comes back to Jesus. Why believe Jesus? Because he rose from the dead. Anyone can make grand claims and argue that they are a special person. But how do they back it up? Jesus backed it up by predicting his resurrection and then being resurrected. If indeed he did this, it gives his opinions substantially more clout with me than, say, that psychic writer my friend believes. In short, part of my belief in the Bible is based on my belief in the resurrection.

So...why do I accept that the resurrection actually occurred? Not just because it is in the Bible—that would be completely circular: "I believe in the Bible because Jesus got up and I believe Jesus got up because it's in the Bible." So why believe in the resurrection? (Before you read on, answer that question: Why do YOU believe in the resurrection of Jesus Christ? Because your parents or pastor or friend told you it was so? Are you piggy-backing on the beliefs of others without owning it yourself?)

Here are some things to mull on:

Totally apart from the Bible, it is evident that something happened around the time of the alleged resurrection of Jesus of

Nazareth. A group of men and women associated with Jesus so believed he was alive that they were willing to die for what they believed. People don't normally die to support a hoax they have perpetrated. They were so convincing in their testimony that many others were likewise convinced and the church grew and continues to grow nearly two millennia later.

If I was to write a book about hockey, and in that book devote a chapter to proving that the greatest player who ever lived was Charlie Chaplin, and in another chapter describe how the team from the Cook Islands in the South Pacific won the 2016 Stanley Cup, and then in yet another chapter expound on the experimental use of exploding pucks in the 1990s to try to make the game more exciting, it would never get published, except possibly as really bad humour. Why? Because it is obviously not true. And many hockey fans alive today know it's not true because they saw what really happened in those eras. There is strong contradictory evidence and a lack of verification of all those false claims.

The historical accounts of Jesus were written at a time, and the resurrection was being proclaimed at a time, when the eyewitnesses of the events were still alive. They talked it up and wrote it down, and many gave their lives taking a stand for what they believed was true. I have never come across an explanation for the transformed lives of the disciples, their passion and courage and martyrdoms, that makes more sense than the resurrection of Jesus.

Additionally, I have seen the power of the name of the resurrected Jesus both in prayer and in direct spiritual warfare, and heard many corresponding reports from others who I know and trust. In short, what I have personally seen and experienced corresponds with who and what the Bible testifies Jesus is.

(For a more thorough look at the arguments and evidence for the resurrection, see Lee Strobel's *The Case for Christ*. Typically when I meet someone who is wrestling with this issue I give them a copy of the book and offer to meet with them and discuss it after they have read it.)

A Christ Follower is truth-based which means Bible-based, in some measure knowing the Bible and also believing it. But there is one final very important component to being Bible based.

Component #3: Apply the Bible

> *"Do not merely listen to the word, and so deceive yourselves. Do what it says... But those who look intently into the perfect law that gives freedom, and continues in it—not forgetting what they have heard but doing it— they will be blessed in what they do." (James 1.22, 25)*

Or as John Maxwell has put it, "Christians know more about the Bible than they ever plan on obeying. We don't need more food; we need more exercise."

Unused truth is as useless as unused muscle. Most of us Christ Followers will state we believe the Bible. We would be a little more reluctant to say we "know" the Bible. After all, few of us have it all memorized. And we would be even more reluctant to say we apply it because we know we don't always apply it fully. Yet being truth-based includes all three. Know it. Believe it. And thirdly, apply it.

To apply the Word means we use it like a ruler—we lay it alongside our lives and say "This is the truth, this is the plumb line, the reference point, I need to adjust myself to it and not ignore the parts I don't like or try to change them." The Bible speaks of being transformed by the renewing of our minds. This happens when we accept the Bible as God's word, take it in through reading and memorization, and then respond to it.

In his book *The Call*, Os Guinness recounts one man's honest response to using the Bible as his reference point:

> *"Thomas Linacre was king's physician to Henry VII and Henry VIII of England, founder of the Royal College of Physicians...*

Late in his life he took Catholic orders and was given a copy of the Gospels to read for the first time. The Bible of course, was still the preserve of the clergy and not in the hands of ordinary people. And Linacre had lived through the darkest of the church's dark hours: the papacy of Alexander VI, the Borgia pope whose bribery, corruption, incest and murder plumbed new depths in the annals of Christian shame.

"Reading the four Gospels for himself, Linacre was amazed and troubled. 'Either these are not the Gospels,' he said, 'or we are not Christians.'"[12]

That's the kind of rigorous honesty we need to bring to our reading of scripture—measuring our own hearts and minds and conduct according to it—versus excusing ourselves and compromising its clear teachings.

If you accept the Bible as God's word, if you get to know it, if you allow it in to do its work in your heart and mind through the Spirit, you will become truth-based, you will develop and grow in this fourth essential character quality of a follower of Jesus Christ.

"Let the message of Christ dwell among you richly as you teach and admonish one another with all wisdom through psalms, hymns and songs from the Spirit, singing to God with gratitude in your hearts." (Colossians 3.16)

In Psalm 19 we have the following rich description of the Word of God:

"The law of the Lord is perfect, refreshing the soul. The statutes of the Lord are trustworthy, making wise the simple. The precepts of the Lord are right, giving joy to the heart. The commands of the Lord are radiant, giving light to the eyes. The fear of the Lord is pure, enduring forever. The ordinances of the Lord are sure

---

12   Os Guinness, *The Call*. Nashville: Word, 1998, 109-10

and all of them are righteous. They are more precious than gold, than much pure gold; they are sweeter than honey, than honey from the honeycomb. By them is your servant warned; in keeping them there is great reward." (Psalm 19.7-11)

A Christ Follower is truth-based, someone who is growing in their knowledge, belief and application of God's rich, powerful and everlasting Word.

CHAPTER 7

Evangelistic

*"But you will receive power when the Holy Spirit
comes on you; and you will be my witnesses in
Jerusalem, and in all Judea and Samaria, and to the
ends of the earth." (Acts 1.8)*

The movie *The Apostle*, starring Robert Duval, begins with his
character Sonny pulling up to a serious multi-vehicle traffic accident with his mother, played by June Carter Cash, in the passenger
seat. Sonny gets out and makes his way to a vehicle that is far off the
road with a young man and woman inside it. The young man is seriously hurt, possibly near death. Sonny prays over the vehicle, turns
off the radio that is still playing, and then calls on the young man
to accept the Lord Jesus Christ as his Saviour. Despite attempts of a
police officer to get him away from the car, he breaks through and
the young man responds to the message Sonny shares. As he leaves
the vehicle, the officer says, "I guess you think you accomplished
something in there, huh?" Sonny replies "I know I did." After a
bit more of an exchange with the officer he goes back to his own
vehicle singing, telling his mother, "We made news in heaven this
mornin'."[13]

If you watch the entire movie with a diverse small group of
people as I have done, some people will identify with, and in some

---

13 *The Apostle*. Alliance Films Inc., 1997. DVD

ways, admire the Sonny character, while others will hate him. But one thing everyone agrees on is that this character clearly had a passion to tell people about Jesus Christ. He desperately wanted people to know that Jesus died to pay the price for their sins and that they could be forgiven. And while he was in many ways very unlike the kind of Christ Follower being described in these pages, in that one very significant way he was like Jesus.

Jesus Christ was and is in the "people business". He didn't come so much to start a new religion as he did to connect with people and reach people and change people. Jesus' first words to his first disciples were, *"Come, follow me, and I will send you out to fish for people."* (Matthew 4 19)

His last recorded words in that same gospel are:

> *"All authority in heaven and earth has been given to me. Therefore go and make disciples of all nations, baptizing them in the name of the Father and of the Son and of the Holy Spirit, and teaching them to obey everything I have commanded you. And surely I am with you always, to the very end of the age."* (Matthew 28.18-20)

He didn't say, "Follow me and you will have a calm and peaceful life, follow me and you will be safe and secure, follow me and you will be a respectable citizen of your city and country", or "follow me and you'll have lots of money." He said, "Follow me and reach out to people. Follow me and you will be involved in bringing a message to men, women and children that will transform them and change their eternal destinies."

Next to being forgiven and transformed yourself, having your own personal eternal destiny changed, one of the most important things a Christ Follower can do is work with Jesus in bringing the message of transformation to others. It is impossible to avoid the fact that Jesus clearly assumed a core aspect of following him would be reaching others. When he called people to follow him he called them to join him in his mission of seeking and saving the lost. As a result, one of the eight non-negotiable traits of a Christ Follower is being evangelistic. A follower of Jesus Christ is evangelistic. This trait is almost as obvious as the first two, loving God and loving people. Jesus Christ was evangelistic; true followers imitate him in this way.

What Does an Evangelistic Person Look Like?

The gospel is good news, and evangelism is sharing the good news of how God has made it possible through Jesus for us to be forgiven and restored to a right relationship with our Creator. Interestingly, the longer we live with our knowledge of the good news, especially those of us who were raised in a church where the gospel was regularly proclaimed, the less revolutionary that gospel can seem to us. But when we share the gospel regularly and see the amazement so many people have when they realize that Jesus died for them, personally, it helps us recognize just how precious and powerful this gift is, with which we have been entrusted.

One of the reasons I initially went to Bible college was to learn to share my faith. Among the many programs I participated in was Evangelism Explosion, also known as EE. As a part of this ministry, teams of three would visit people who had visited the church and share a fairly comprehensive presentation of the gospel with them.

One week, our team went to visit a man named Grant who lived in the inner city. He wasn't home, but when we went back the following week, there he was ready for us, dressed up in his best, with tea and juice and cookies waiting. His neighbor, who we had bumped into in the hallway of the apartment the previous week, had told him we'd dropped by and he was hoping we would come over again at the same time.

After a little chit chat, I launched into the EE presentation which included a fairly thorough explanation of the "bad news"— the fact that God is holy and we are not, and just how serious that fact is. As I worked my way through that portion of the presentation, describing what sin was and how thoroughly sinful we all are, Grant became more and more agitated until he finally interrupted me and said, "I know I'm a sinner! I know I need forgiveness! How do I get it?!?"

His outburst threw me off my memorized spiel, but I wasn't too distracted to realize that maybe it was time to shift gears to the "good news" part of the presentation and explain who Jesus is and what he came to do. Grant soaked it up like a dry sponge. When it came time to ask if he wanted to respond, to put his faith in Christ, he eagerly responded. When we were done praying together Grant had visibly changed. It wasn't just that he was no longer agitated or nervous. He was the picture of peace. There was a glow about him, a genuine smile, a calmness and confidence, a newness. It was like the spiritual change he'd just experienced had spilled over to the physical and he was reborn on every level.

Grant was the first person I had the opportunity to walk with through that moment of repentance and faith and salvation, and as much as it changed Grant, it also changed me. It reminded me just how relevant, powerful, radical and essential the Gospel is. And it moved me further down the path of becoming an evangelistic follower of Jesus Christ.

What does it mean to be evangelistic? Another personal evangelism training I've found helpful and effective is, "Becoming a Contagious Christian," which is based on a book of the same title. I like that word "contagious" when applied to passionate followers of Jesus Christ. It's like they have a disease, in this case a good disease, and are trying to spread it and hopefully create a pandemic! If being a follower of Jesus was a disease, would you be considered infected? Are you evangelistic? Are you a contagious Christian? Let's take a look at some "symptoms" of that disease and show how we can become more thoroughly infected, more evangelistic.

An Evangelistic Person Values Individuals

"One of the magnificent late 19th century British military expeditions conquered no new lands for Queen Victoria. You won't find it mentioned in the standard history books, but because of the monumental logistics, military historians compare the landing in Ethiopia in 1868 to the Allies' invasion of France in 1944.

"In 1868 Emperor Theodore III of Ethiopia held a group of 53 European captives (30 adults and 23 children), including some missionaries, in a remote, 9,000-foot high bastion deep in the interior. Among them were a British consul and a special diplomatic emissary sent to secure the release of the prisoners. By letter, Queen Victoria pleaded in vain with Theodore to release the captives. Finally, the government ordered a full-scale military expedition from India to march into Ethiopia—not to conquer the country and make it a British colony, but simply to rescue a tiny band of civilians who had suffered in prison for more than four years.

"The invasion force included 32,000 men, heavy artillery, and 44 elephants to carry the big guns. Provisions included 50,000 tons of beef and pork and 30,000 gallons of rum. Engineers built landing piers, water treatment plants, a railroad, and telegraph line to the interior, plus many bridges. All of this to fight one decisive battle, after which the prisoners were released, and everyone packed up and went home."[14]

In Luke 15, Jesus tells three related stories to show what God thinks of people. He told them in response to the religious people of the day who had a problem with him hanging out with the dregs of society.

---

14 Jim Reapsome, *Release the Captives*, Current Thoughts and Trends, NavPress, May 1999

> *"Now the tax collectors and sinners were all gathering around to hear Jesus. But the Pharisees and the teachers of the law muttered, 'This man welcomes sinners and eats with them.'" (Luke 15.1-2)*

In response, Jesus told the stories of the lost sheep, the lost coin and the lost or prodigal son. A shepherd loses one sheep, leaves the ninety nine that are safe and goes and finds the lost one. A woman loses a coin so she cleans her house from top to bottom until she finds it. A man's son leaves with his early inheritance. When he finally returns home broke and broken, the father embraces him and throws a party.

The first mark of an evangelistic person is that they value individuals, they value other people. And that value is not merely a value of the flesh and blood, the physical wellbeing of that person. It goes beyond the physical here and now to recognizing the eternal value of the individual. If you think Queen Victoria's expedition was disproportionately big and expensive, look at God's expedition to rescue us: God became flesh, and died, so we could live. What does that tell us about God's attitude toward people?

> *"God our Savior…wants all people to be saved and to come to a knowledge of the truth." (1 Timothy 2.4)*

> *"Instead he is patient with you, not wanting anyone to perish, but everyone to come to repentance." (2 Peter 3.9)*

> *"For God so loved the world that he gave his one and only Son, that whoever believes in him shall not perish but have eternal life." (John 3.16)*

If we can grasp how much God values people, how much he loves us—and if we can be captured by that same kind of love, concern and passion for the eternal destiny of other people—then we are on track to gaining this essential trait of a Christ Follower. And if we don't, we likely won't become evangelistic. A biblical follower of

Jesus Christ is captured and carried along by God's heart for people. They are infected with the love of God for everyone, a love that will do anything to save them.

An Evangelistic Person Lives a Distinct, Redemptive Lifestyle

An unsettling observation I've heard regarding evangelism is that when we invite someone to become a follower of Jesus, one of their considerations is whether or not they want to be like us. What unsettles me is the idea that someone might reject Jesus not because of who he is but because of who I am, or who another "Christian" they have interacted with is.

> *"You are the salt of the earth. But if the salt loses its saltiness, how can it be made salty again? It is no longer good for anything, except to be thrown out and trampled underfoot. You are the light of the world. A city on a hill cannot be hidden. Neither do people light a lamp and put it under a bowl. Instead they put it on its stand, and it gives light to everyone in the house. In the same way, let your light shine before others, that they may see your good deeds and glorify your Father in heaven." (Matthew 5.13-16)*

God's people as individuals and as a group—the church—are to relate to the surrounding culture as salt and light. Another similar metaphor is that of perfume, where the Apostle Paul speaks of God using us *"to spread the aroma of the knowledge of him everywhere."* (2 Corinthians 2.14). Each of these pictures highlights the need to be appropriately distinct, but also strategically involved and making a difference wherever God places us in our cultures. And so the second mark of an evangelistic Christ Follower is living a distinct, redemptive lifestyle.

Among other things, this ought to bring back thoughts of holiness, the third trait we looked at. By "redemptive" I mean a lifestyle that contributes to the cause of Christ, brings about positive change in the cultures and subcultures in which we participate and foreshadows the Kingdom.

Some people are distinctively selfish or immoral. Christ Followers are called to be distinct in the opposite direction. The New Testament is full of descriptions of what it means to live as a disciple of Jesus. The character qualities in this book describe some of those differences. According to Titus 2, the way we live should make the gospel attractive. Attractive, not repulsive. But please note, this does not require perfection!

I occasionally have people tell me about Christians they've dealt with in business who took them to the cleaners, or Christian neighbors who did something especially nasty. But I've never had anyone complain that they knew a Christian who wasn't perfect. God doesn't expect us to be perfect this side of eternity and no one else does either. But they do expect, and God expects, us to be positively distinct.

If you consider yourself a Christian and you are not living in a Christlike manner, if you blend in seamlessly with the culture, like a chameleon taking on the look of whatever context it's in, then perhaps the most evangelistic thing you can do is take a vow of silence. Don't tell anyone you are a Christian since that might only serve to inoculate them against the one truth that can save them.

One of the most painful moments in my high school years was a report my best friend brought to me. He had been in a group talking and my name came up and someone said "Isn't he a Christian?" And another fellow, a friend who had known me for years laughed and said, "Wride? Are you kidding? He's not a Christian." When my friend reported this incident it shook me up—I knew I wasn't an angel, but I didn't think I was so bad that my longtime friend didn't even consider me a Christian. It rattled me so much that it played a part in getting me back on track with the Lord.

As Os Guinness has noted: *"The problem is not that God's people aren't where they should be, but that they aren't what they should be, right where they are."* We cannot be effective in evangelism without a redemptive, distinctive lifestyle.

An Evangelistic Person Works to Be Ready

Early in my life as a pastor, I came to a surprising (to me) conclusion: I realized that it was possible for people to be lifelong church goers (and in those days that often meant two services on Sunday, plus Sunday school and a midweek gathering), committed Christians, and even have a passion for seeing people come to faith in Jesus, but not know how to share their faith. This wasn't simply a weakness in the church I pastored, but a systemic problem that I would have seen in the churches of my pre-pastor days if I had been paying attention. This also revealed a systemic weakness in the way pastors were (and perhaps still are) trained, and a problem with the expectations placed on them by denominational officials, local church boards and members of the congregation. Few seem to be asking the question, "Are people being equipped to participate with Jesus in his seeking and saving of the lost?"

> *"But in your hearts revere Christ as Lord. Always be prepared to give an answer to everyone who asks you to give the reason for the hope that you have. But do this with gentleness and respect..."* (1 Peter 3.15)

Preparation implies action. Preparation implies work. Another mark of an evangelistic Christ Follower is that they work to be ready. When an opportunity comes to share the gospel, they are ready. In time, with training, they not only see and take opportunities, they create them.

A big part of being ready is an ability to clearly articulate the gospel message. Can you describe in simple terms the story of Jesus, who he is, what he did, and how a person can receive the forgiveness

God offers through him? Can you describe in clear terms how you came to believe that he died for you and rose from the grave, and what has happened in your life since that time that shows evidence of his power? And can you do this for someone who has not been churched in any way, who has little or no understanding of the basic story of the Bible or Jesus Christ? In the past, evangelistic efforts and training could focus on unsaved church people, and be very fruitful—there were a lot of them! There are still a lot of these people in churches, but we are now increasingly dealing with the thoroughly unchurched, including those who grew up under other religions or have created their own a-la-carte belief system.

Here's the challenge I often lay before other believers: We need to be ready and able to share what Jesus has done for us personally, and what he has done and wants to do for everyone. Very few people can effectively communicate these things without some prior thought and some prior deliberate preparation. But why should it surprise us that preparation is required to do the most important task on earth? We prepare for holidays, retirement, weddings, and many other life events. We also need to prepare for sharing Christ. This requires pastors, churches, denominations and congregations with the humility to realize they need to change the way they are functioning and truly equip people for service, including evangelism.

In addition to training, an important part of working to be ready is intercession. In fact, so significant is the discipline of prayer when it comes to evangelism that I considered making prayer for the lost an entirely separate mark of an evangelistic Christ Follower. Prayer for those who need to be reached flows from a sense of the deep value of each person, a sense of our own need for help in sharing the gospel, and recognition that when we share Christ we aren't ultimately engaging in a logical argument or a marketing exercise, but in a spiritual battle that requires spiritual strength and weaponry.

A passage I often use as a pattern to pray for those I am called to reach is from Paul's account of his mission before Agrippa. He receives his commission on the road to Damascus, after he's been knocked off his horse. Jesus is speaking; he tells Paul he is being sent to the Gentiles and then says:

> "I am sending you to open their eyes and turn them
> from darkness to light, and from the power of Satan to
> God, so that they may receive forgiveness of sins and
> a place among those who are sanctified by faith in me."
> (Acts 26.18)

Using the ideas in this passage I will pray for individuals or groups of people, asking the Lord to open their eyes, to turn them from darkness to light, and from the power of Satan to God, so that they can receive forgiveness of sins and a place among those sanctified by faith in Jesus. And I often supplement it with prayer for myself in keeping with Paul's prayer requests for himself, to *"declare it fearlessly, as I should"* (Ephesians 6.20) and *"that I may proclaim it clearly, as I should."* (Colossians 4.4)

I am concerned that people sometimes think this is hyperbole, but I truly believe it: At least half the work of evangelism is intercession. It's fascinating, fun and occasionally scary to see what happens in people's lives as you pray for "their eyes to be opened," etc. It's surprising to see those who seemed disinterested in spiritual things, or spiritual people disinterested in Christianity, begin to get interested and ask questions about the faith or say things like, "Do you think it would be alright if I came to church sometime?" (Yes, our culture is so unchurched that many people don't even know if they are free to wander into a church service without permission!) And it can be a little scary, as you pray for people, to see the crises that come into their lives, stripping away their self-sufficiency, leaving them desperate for outside help.

As I write this chapter, my wife Kristin has been having increasingly focused and prolonged conversations (often via text messages) with a co-worker who has become a friend. This woman is intensely seeking on multiple levels in her life, and has seen in Kristin a calmness, stability and kindness that she craves. Kristin often prays with and for her at work about her challenges, has made herself available to talk any time of the day or night, and, of course intercedes for her faithfully. One evening recently she got a text from her friend asking for a Bible verse that might relate to a current situation in her life. I asked Kristin, "She's basically begging for the Gospel—when are you going to share it with her?!" Kristin told me the time would come but not yet. Of course she has been sharing the gospel in snippets and living a redemptive, distinct life as an agent of Jesus Christ for this woman all along. Based on what I have seen many times in the past, I expect that this woman will come to know Jesus through coming to know Kristin, from being bathed in intercession, from exposure to the Word and from experiencing the resulting work of the Spirit of God in her life circumstances. (Update: Since I first wrote this Kristin's friend has come to faith and been baptized.)

An evangelistic person works to be ready for evangelistic opportunities by preparing and praying.

An Evangelistic Person Makes Sacrifices and Takes Risks

An evangelistic follower of Jesus values people, lives a redemptive distinct lifestyle, works to be ready, and finally, makes sacrifices and takes risks in order to share the good news.

Early in my pastoral ministry, in a small town in northern Canada, I bumped into a fellow named Mike in the hospital. Mike was about 80 years old. As we talked, we discovered to the amazement of both of us that he was the maternal grandfather of one of my best friends from my teenage years, a fellow named Dan, who had been my canoe racing partner. We'd gone to the National Championships for marathon canoe racing, winning a silver and a gold medal in three appearances.

Due to a family breakdown years before—he and Dan's grandmother had divorced and she had remarried—he hadn't seen or talked to Dan or his family for a very long time. I brought Mike some pictures from my canoe racing days with Dan. When I showed him the pictures he got teary eyed and couldn't thank me enough. Now I can be a little slow, but I was sharp enough to realize that this wasn't a mere coincidence, this was what we call a "divine appointment" —something that looks like a coincidence but is obviously orchestrated by God. After all, I was serving in a small community of two thousand people, 1300 km away from where I had grown up, two provinces away! I knew immediately that I was supposed to share the gospel with Mike.

Mike got out of the hospital and went back to his home about 30 miles west of the town where I lived. I often had to drive by his place on my way to a larger community, so I frequently stopped for a coffee and a visit. For some reason I found it harder than usual to turn the conversation with Mike to spiritual things. I didn't feel like I was making much progress. Occasionally I drove right by and told myself I'd stop next time. The non-visits increased in frequency. At one point a few months passed and I didn't visit him. Then for about a two week period I had a strong urging to call him.

I put it off until one day I just decided to phone and see if I could drop by for a visit. His wife answered the phone. I asked to speak with Mike. She said, "Who is this?" I told her and she bluntly stated, "Mike died last week."

I was stunned. I felt sick as I hung up the phone, and still do when I think of it. And in case you don't understand what the big deal is, let me put it in plain English: Mike died, as far as I know, without faith in Jesus Christ, which means he is separated from God forever. And he was my assignment. I understood that the day I discovered our connection through Dan. I was the one, perhaps not the first one, but likely the last one the Spirit of God directed to share Jesus with him. And, as far as I know, I failed.

I wish that was the only story I have like this one, but there are several other situations, not necessarily as dramatic, where I had opportunity to share with someone, didn't, and they have since died.

Unlike my example in that story, a disciple of Jesus Christ, an evangelistic person, makes sacrifices and takes risks to share Christ. The sacrifice might be time or money, the risk might be embarrassment or rejection. But those are sacrifices, those are risks an evangelistic person is prepared to take. This sacrificial, risk-taking posture flows naturally from loving and valuing people, from knowing that they have an inherent eternal value. Given the stakes, the cost is small and the risk is minimal.

> *"To the weak I became weak, to win the weak. I have*
> *become all things to all people so that by all possible*
> *means I might save some." (1 Corinthians 9.22)*

Paul is saying, in essence, "Whatever it takes, short of moral compromise, I will do to connect with people and create an opportunity to share the Gospel."

An evangelistic individual or church makes sacrifices and takes risks to share the gospel. There is risk and sacrifice when we make evangelism a corporate priority. But there is an added power and effectiveness when we do it together.

Other marks could be added, including some of the other DNA character qualities, which contribute to evangelism. But when you look at the things highlighted in this chapter, what do you conclude? Are you an evangelistic person, a "contagious" follower of the One who seeks and saves the lost?

Here are some simple steps to take in growing in this character quality:

1. Begin praying regularly, at least weekly if you don't already, for two or more people you believe the Lord has brought into your life for you to share Jesus with. It may be a relative, a neighbor, or a co-worker. If you are a Christ Follower there are people like that in your life. Pray for God to reveal them to you, and then pray for them. As soon as you start praying, watch for the opportunities that will rise up to share Christ with some of them.

2. If you haven't been trained in personal evangelism, if you can't clearly and concisely share the story of what Jesus Christ has done for you and how another person can receive his forgiveness, make that a priority for this year. Commit yourself to being

trained. Your church or a church near you may offer a training program, and there are assorted parachurch training opportunities as well. With online access to information and training from churches and organizations around the world, it is quite easy to learn how to share your faith effectively.

3. One of my passions is communication, including public speaking. As a result I have often participated in Toastmaster clubs in the communities I've pastored in. A Toastmasters club is the closest thing to a small group that I have seen outside the church. People get to know each other very well because they are always giving speeches about themselves or areas of passion and interest. In every club I've been a part of, people I have gotten to know, and have interceded for, have come to faith in Jesus Christ. No, I haven't always been the one to "bring them across the line", but I have been privileged to be a part of their journey. People have asked to come to church or simply shown up in church because they knew me from the club. The truth is, I've never really gone to Toastmasters to share my faith and convert people—I've gone because I wanted to refine my public speaking. But by getting myself out of the comfortable Christian circles and away from the busyness of church life where I can meet people who need Jesus, there is at least a chance for evangelism to occur.

Here's the point: Harness your interests and passions to build relationships with people who need Jesus. It could be speaking, or quilting, or running, or canoeing, or comic books, or orchids, or pretty much anything.

I used to do a lot of coyote hunting to supplement our meagre small-town, small church pastor's income. I'd sell the hides and then buy a set of blinds or some tires for the car. Don't get me wrong—I enjoyed it because it gave me something to do on my days off through the long cold winter, and it was a nice throwback to my earlier years when I'd trapped fulltime, paying for my first year of Bible college with fur money. Eventually, as word got out about my coyote hunting, people began phoning the church about problem animals. My favorite phone call of all time came from a rancher. I answered the phone and he said, "Are you the preacher who shoots coyotes? I'm having problems with 'em. Can you come out and kill a few?" Two men started coming to that church due in part to my hunting on their land. (In addition, it messed with the heads of many other non-church people about what a pastor was, and that was reward in itself!) In a church I later pastored, one man told me he came because he had heard I hunted, and, as a result, hoped I could relate to him, as he had the same passion for the outdoors.

Anything you love to do (that is legal and moral!) can be an avenue for redemptive contact with people and can ultimately lead to evangelism. Additionally, involvement in events and organizations that are not a part of the church world allows us to participate in the cultural transformation that is also part of the Gospel and the extension of the Kingdom. So, get trained, start doing the things you love with a heart open to those you will get to know who need to meet your Saviour. Begin to pray for them. Then get ready to take the opportunities the Spirit of God will orchestrate for you to share the good news.

A Christ Follower is evangelistic—valuing people, displaying a distinct redemptive lifestyle, preparing to share their faith, taking risks and making sacrifices for opportunities to share the Gospel.

CHAPTER 8

Persevering

"We often suffer, but we are never crushed. Even when we don't know what to do, we never give up. In times of trouble, God is with us, and when we are knocked down, we get up again." (2 Corinthians 4.8-9, CEV) [15]

What does it take for you to quit? My fourth year out of high school was a year of change for me. When I'd graduated from high school I began what I saw as an ideal, "dream come true" life: Trapping from September to Christmas, cutting survey lines in the wilderness from New Year's until spring, and then canoe racing through to the end of August or beginning of September. Early in my fourth year out of high school I decided that I would go west to Bible college for a year "to get my head straight," and then take life from there. At the same time, my canoeing partner Dan was planning to go east to Ontario for school. We knew it might be our last year of racing, so we wanted to go out with a bang.

We quit our winter mineral exploration jobs at the end of March and drove south and west until we found some open water for training. Where we lived in northern Manitoba the lakes were usually

---

15 Contemporary English Version® Copyright © 1995 American Bible Society. All rights reserved.

covered with ice until sometime in May. So we trained for a month in southern Alberta and British Columbia. And we trained hard—running, long hours of paddling and a stringent athletic diet. One older experienced racer we met on that trip told us, "Make sure you rest as hard as you train." We nodded in agreement, but thought to ourselves, "Yeah, an old guy like that might need to rest, but we want to train!"

We came second in our first race of the year, which was a bit disappointing considering the hard training we'd done. The night before our second race we had a fight—not an argument but a fight. No punches were thrown, but the next day we were so tired from our extended, hostile wrestling match that we could hardly paddle. We didn't do very well in that race. The following week was our home town race, The Flin Flon Trout Festival Gold Rush Canoe Derby for the Labatt Trophy. (Locals simply called it The Gold Rush.) The first day we did quite well since there were more than three miles of portages in the 27-mile course, and we were as fast as anyone on land carrying a canoe.

Unfortunately, it was a canoe-paddling race, not a canoe-carrying race. The second day of the three-day race was almost entirely on water. We had a strong start, but as the day wore on it felt like we had an anchor tied to our canoe. We later realized we had severely over-trained, due to our failure to take the veteran racer's advice. Our bodies desperately needed rest and recovery. As the race wore on, team after team passed us. And then something terrible happened, something that had never happened to us before, even in our novice years. It was devastating, demoralizing and inconceivable to our young male minds: We were passed by a women's team! And while it's funny to look back and laugh at our crushed egos, believe me, it wasn't funny at the time.

When that leg of the race ended we simply picked up our canoe, loaded it on the pickup and drove home. The next day at the starting line, the third and final day of the race began and we weren't there. That was the last time Dan and I raced together. So much for going out with a bang. We'd quit our last race together. And while

DNA of a Christ Follower

there were many contributing factors, it was that moment of being passed by a women's team that finally did us in.

What does it take for you to quit?

In Matthew 24 Jesus is responding to his disciples' questions regarding the end of the age:

> "Then you will be handed over to be persecuted and put to death, and you will be hated by all nations because of me. At that time many will turn away from the faith and will betray and hate each other, and many false prophets will appear and deceive many people. Because of the increase of wickedness, the love of most will grow cold, but whoever stands firm to the end will be saved." (Matthew 24.9-13)

What about the one who doesn't stand firm?

In Hebrews it says "You need to persevere so that when you have done the will of God, you will receive what he has promised." (Hebrews 10.36)

And if you don't persevere...?

Maybe your answer to those questions is the same as mine: "I don't know and I don't plan to find out!"

In his conclusion to the Parable of the Sower in Luke, Jesus explains, "But the seed on good soil stands for those with a noble and good heart, who hear the word, retain it, and by persevering produce a crop." (Luke 8.15)

The earlier verses explain some of the alternatives to perseverance. And each of these passages communicates a key biblical fact about perseverance: Perseverance is essential. In other words, just as a disciple of Jesus Christ is someone who loves God and loves people, is holy and growing in holiness, truth-based and evangelistic, just as basic, just as essential is this trait of perseverance. A Christ Follower is persevering. Why is perseverance essential for the Christ Follower? Can't we simply rest in the fact that we are saved, kick back and wait for Jesus to show up?

Perseverance is Essential
Because We're Still in the Race

In 1953, the battle was on to see who would be the first runner to run a mile in under four minutes, with several runners getting within three seconds of the goal. Finally on May 6, 1954, Roger Bannister did it in 3:59.4. On June 21 of the same year John Landy ran it in 3:58, which of course became the set up for an historic meeting between the two.

Their big race against each other took place on August 7, 1954 at the Commonwealth Games in Vancouver, Canada. Landy led for most of the race, up to ten yards at one point, but with 90 yards to go he looked over his left shoulder precisely as Bannister was accelerating for his final kick and passing him on the right. The momentum shift of that instant carried Bannister across the line first, though both men were under four minutes. Landy told a reporter from Time magazine that if he hadn't looked back he would have won. In 1967 a bronze sculpture commemorating the pivotal moment of the race was unveiled in Vancouver, leading Landy to comment "While Lot's wife was turned into a pillar of salt for looking back, I am probably the only one ever turned into bronze for looking back."

The account of this great moment in sports history illustrates why perseverance is essential for the follower of Jesus Christ: Perseverance is essential because we're still in the race. The race doesn't end when you repent and receive Jesus Christ, it doesn't end when you are baptized, it doesn't end when you complete your church's discipleship program or graduate with a theological degree, it doesn't end when you turn 20 or 40 or 65 or 105.

I am continually challenged by Paul's summary of his persevering posture in life and ministry:

> "Do you not know that in a race all the runners run,
> but only one gets the prize? Run in such a way as to
> get the prize. Everyone who competes in the games
> goes into strict training. They do it to get a crown that
> will not last; but we do it to get a crown that will last

forever. Therefore I do not run like someone running aimlessly; I do not fight like a boxer beating the air. No, I strike a blow to my body and make it my slave so that after I have preached to others, I myself will not be disqualified for the prize." (I Corinthians 9.24-27)

Later, he was able to say, just before he died:

"I have fought the good fight, I have finished the race, I have kept the faith. Now there is in store for me the crown of righteousness, which the Lord, the righteous Judge, will award to me on that day—and not only to me, but also to all who have longed for his appearing." (2 Timothy 4.7-8)

That's the goal, that's the target of this character quality- to finish the race and get the "well done" at the end.

Perseverance is essential because we haven't yet finished the race. But there is another reason perseverance is essential.

Perseverance is Essential Because There Will Be Difficulties

Maybe when you came to Christ you were inadvertently lied to by some well-meaning person who led you to believe that if you became a Christian everything would be fine, that life would be like riding a lightweight bicycle downhill on a paved highway. Maybe since you've come to Christ you've read authors or heard speakers who indicate that if you live a certain way, give your money a certain way, that if you do things right, you will have a healthy, wealthy, basically problem-free Christian life. The truth is, if you signed up for a Christian life with no problems, you didn't sign up for the life Jesus offers, you didn't sign up to be a Christ Follower.

"Brother will betray brother to death, and a father his child; children will rebel against their parents and have

*them put to death. Everyone will hate you because of
me, but those who stand firm to the end will be saved."
(Matthew 10.21-22)*

*"In fact, everyone who wants to live a godly life in
Christ Jesus will be persecuted..." (2 Timothy 3.12)*

Everyone. It's normal. It's to be expected. The Christian life is a war zone. I Peter tells us not to be surprised when we suffer for following Christ, but to expect it.

The fact that we need perseverance implies that there will be difficulties, and scripture backs up this assumption. Which is the second reason perseverance is essential: Perseverance is essential because there will be difficulties.

Jesus told his followers and prospective followers, *"Whoever wants to be my disciple must deny themselves and take up their cross and follow me."* (Mark 8.34) Jesus didn't mislead anyone; he was up front. "If you follow me they will hate you. If you follow me there will be huge trials. If you want to follow me," he said right from the start, "Take up your cross." In other words, be prepared to persevere even to the point of death.

You may be aware of the rampant persecution of Christians going on around the world today. As I write this, a cursory look online reveals:

- Christians in Bangladesh are being ordered to stop building a church, with threats of beatings if they continue
- Roughly forty people, including pregnant women and young children, have been murdered in Niger during attacks on Christian villages
- A pastor in China has been tied up and hauled away by authorities, with no news three weeks later as to his location or condition
- Indonesian churches are being sealed up or torn down
- Christians in Laos have been told to renounce their faith or lose their land and livestock.

If you go online today you will find new stories about the persecutions of Christ Followers around the world. Amazingly, even in such situations, while some Christians do renounce their faith, many more stand firm. This corroborates the second basic fact about perseverance that we find in scripture, which is that perseverance is always possible.

Perseverance is Always Possible

Yes, when following Christ becomes dangerous or uncomfortable, some do throw in the towel, lay down their cross and stop following Jesus. In fact, in our soft, flabby, Westernized version of Christianity, some people quit due to things that can hardly be called trials and tribulations, much less persecutions. I've seen financial downturns, failing health, even suffering caused by foolish and sinful choices, shake the faith of individuals. Some people give up even though they still believe the gospel in some measure, because they see that the world offers more immediate pleasure and an easier way of living for a time—which is true, there is pleasure in sin for a season—so they wander off. But no matter how bad things have gotten, no matter how intense persecution has become in history or in the present, there have always been those who stood firm, who persevered, who took up their crosses and followed Jesus, even to the death when necessary.

Yes, perseverance is always possible. Let's take a look at some of the "means of perseverance," some things that help make perseverance possible.

"For everything that was written in the past was written to teach us, so that through the endurance taught in the Scriptures and the encouragement they provide we might have hope. May the God who gives endurance and encouragement give you the same attitude of mind toward each other that Christ Jesus had, so that with one mind

and one voice you may glorify the God and Father of our
Lord Jesus Christ." (Romans 15.4-6)

Perseverance, according to this short but rich passage, comes
from looking at God's work in the past, especially as recorded in
his word, and in fact from God himself. He is the "God who gives
endurance..."

> "Remember those earlier days after you had received
> the light, when you endured in a great conflict full
> of suffering. Sometimes you were publicly exposed to
> insult and persecution; at other times you stood side
> by side with those who were so treated. You suffered
> along with those in prison and joyfully accepted the
> confiscation of your property, because you knew that
> you yourselves had better and lasting possessions. So
> do not throw away your confidence; it will be richly
> rewarded. You need to persevere so that when you
> have done the will of God, you will receive what he
> has promised." (Hebrews 10.32-36)

Here we see that perseverance comes from looking ahead, from
taking the eternal perspective, which by the way foreshadows a trait
yet to be revealed.

And then we have this well-known but important passage on the
topic of perseverance:

> "Therefore, since we are surrounded by such a great
> cloud of witnesses, let us throw off everything that
> hinders and the sin that so easily entangles. And let
> us run with perseverance the race marked out for us,
> fixing our eyes on Jesus, the pioneer and perfecter of
> faith. For the joy set before him he endured the cross,
> scorning its shame, and sat down at the right hand of
> the throne of God. Consider him who endured such

opposition from sinners, so that you will not grow weary and lose heart." (Hebrews 12.1-3)

There are two steps given to us here for perseverance. But just before we look at the steps, note how the command is stated: "Let us…And let us…" Like all the other traits we are exploring, there is certainly a personal component, but there is also a community component. We don't do it alone; we don't develop or live out a given character quality alone; we do it together.

Perseverance is Possible
When We Throw Off the Baggage

With that important qualification, the first step in persevering is throwing off the baggage that interferes in our Christian life. It comes from dealing with sin as well as those things that may not be sin, but that bog us down. This might help us understand why people even in relatively persecution-free parts of the world still quit the Christian life. It's not just because of the problems or difficulties they face, it's because they are so loaded down with other baggage that when difficulty comes it drains their last reserves. If you want to persevere, get rid of the things that bog you down.

With my background in canoe racing, I love canoe trips. One of the benefits of traveling in the wilderness with a canoe is that you can pack a lot of gear—especially if you have few portages—and camp very comfortably. But when you go on a backpacking trip and have to carry all the gear on your person, you pack far less. You don't bring that extra blanket, multiple fishing rods, or the large cooler full of drinks and meat. In fact, back-packing is such a different, stripped down form of wilderness travel compared to canoeing that my standard reply when asked to go on extended multi-day hiking trips is "It's against my religion."

However, just this past summer, a friend named Kelly asked me to do the West Coast Trail on Vancouver Island with him and his two teenage boys. Since I didn't want to spend a lot of money on hiking gear that I might never use again, I simply used a lot of my canoe trip gear, including a five-pound tent, five-pound sleeping bag and five-pound mattress. Good premium hiking gear could have reduced that fifteen pounds to about five pounds total. I also packed too much food, and food that was heavier than necessary. As a result, my pack for the one week trip weighed sixty pounds when it could have weighed forty-five or so. With some sets of ladders on the deep valley walls approaching two hundred rungs down, and another two hundred up, with mile after mile of roots and mud in the rain forest and loose sand on the beach, every pound was significant. Kelly and I paid a lot of attention to and quizzed other hikers about their gear and how we could lighten our packs, just in case we were ever to do a similar hike in the future.

Getting rid of spiritual baggage is much the same as packing for a hike. You leave behind what you don't need or what will interfere with your forward progress.

In one of my files I have four very official-looking pieces of paper that for me are a source of both regret—a permanent reminder of my imperfection—but also a source of comfort. As I neared the end of my Bible schooling and looked toward becoming a pastor, I had a very light course load and ended up spending a lot of time in the Word and in prayer. I was determined to enter the pastorate with no spiritual baggage, no unconfessed or undealt-with sin. One issue kept coming up in my mind, but I didn't know how to deal with it. Finally, I concluded I had to do something.

So, after final exams in the spring, with just a summer of work and one more fall semester to complete my degree, I went down to the Canada Employment Center in my city, walked up to the girl at the desk and said, "Several summers ago I was drawing Unemployment Insurance, and I feel I abused the system and I want to pay it back." She stared at me in silence for a moment. Then she called her supervisor, I repeated my spiel and he stared at me with disbelief before instructing me to sit down for a while. He came back, took me into his office, and took notes while I shared my concerns.

I explained to him how that particular summer, after working through the winter in mineral exploration, I'd had no intention of finding a job because I was too busy canoe racing. Additionally, I had not declared the money I'd won that summer canoe racing as income. Two breaches of the requirements for receiving unemployment benefits: not looking for work and not reporting income. The man I was talking with worked very hard to convince me I had really done nothing wrong. He said that winnings aren't really earnings and that I couldn't have found a job that would come close to matching my winter income anyway. He concluded by explaining that even if I had done wrong, there was no way to get the money back into the system. His final words to me were "Just don't do it again!" I said, "Don't worry about that!"

I had gone in prepared to cough up a few thousand dollars, possibly at the expense of being able to do my final semester of college that fall. But I left as I had come in, except that now I had a completely clear, baggage-free conscience.

For many Christ Followers, shedding unnecessary baggage requires making, or at least attempting to make restitution for past wrongs. I've both experienced and heard many stories of the freedom and "lightness" and release and joy that comes from making things right. Revivalist teaching and many discipleship programs of the not-too-distant past emphasized this need for making things right, a biblical principle that is now an often overlooked application of "throwing off the baggage that interferes with our Christian lives."

Perseverance is Possible
When We Fix Our Eyes on Jesus

The second step given in Hebrews 12 for preserving is a call to fix our eyes on Jesus, to consider him and what he went through. The 2004 movie, *The Passion of the Christ*, did this for many people. In graphic, some would say too graphic detail, it communicated the suffering and death of Christ.

"We've been surrounded and battered by troubles, but we're not demoralized; we're not sure what to do, but we know that God knows what to do; we've been spiritually terrorized, but God hasn't left our side; we've been thrown down, but we haven't broken. What they did to Jesus, they do to us—trial and torture, mockery and murder; what Jesus did among them, he does in us—he lives! Our lives are at constant risk for Jesus' sake, which makes Jesus' life all the more evident in us." (2 Corinthians 4.8-10) [16]

That isn't just a "rah rah" psyche-up passage that provides no real practical help. In fact, it shares what is a real possibility for all Christ Followers who fix their eyes on Jesus.

The world-famous Boston Marathon is neither the most difficult nor the most hill-intensive footrace, though being a marathon, it is still a significant challenge. But one feature that makes it more difficult than it otherwise would be is Heartbreak Hill. Heartbreak is the last of four hills known as the Newton hills, which begin at mile 16 in the race. The final hill shows up at the 20.5-mile mark and though it is not overly long (.4 mile/600 meters) or a huge elevation gain (27 meters/88 feet), at this point the runners have faced several long downhill segments, straining their quadriceps, they've climbed the three prior hills, and now, just as they have likely depleted their glycogen reserves and are possibly "hitting the wall," Heartbreak rears its ugly head. The combination of its location and its elevation pushes runners to the limit, some even to the point of quitting.

Like you, I have met many people in the middle of Heartbreak Hill, facing a severe test of their faith. And, possibly like you, I have found myself fighting to stay in the race while everything in me seemed to be screaming "Quit!" in order to end the pain. Perhaps you find yourself there right now.

---

16 Scripture taken from *THE MESSAGE*, Copyright © 1993, 1994, 1995, 1996, 2000, 2001, 2002. Used by permission of NavPress Publishing Group

It's not that someone is holding a gun to your head calling you to deny Jesus Christ. That might actually look appealing in the face of what you seem to be facing. And you don't know if you can make it. Read this carefully with yours eyes and heart: Based on the Word of God, the truth is you can make it. Perseverance is always possible. You can make it.

Perseverance is Possible Because of Who God Is

A speaker at a pastor and spouse retreat my wife and I once attended made this statement: "God's grace is effective in any situation not because of what it finds in that situation, but because of what it brings to the situation." In other words, perseverance is always possible not because of who you are, or how tough you can be, or how deep you can dig down and find more personal resources. Perseverance is always possible because of who God is, his faithfulness to us, and what he brings to our circumstances.

> (Jesus said) "My sheep listen to my voice; I know them, and they follow me. I give them eternal life, and they shall never perish; no one will snatch them out of my hand. My Father, who has given them to me, is greater than all; no one can snatch them out of my Father's hand." (John 10.27-29)

Yes, perseverance is essential. But always remember it is also possible. Why? Because, as with all directives to us in scripture, God doesn't just tell us to do something and then leave us blowing in the wind. God says, "You must persevere!" And then, just as quickly, he says, "Here, let me give you perseverance." He says "Hang on to me! And by the way, I'm hanging on to you."

I'm a hobby mineral prospector—have been as long as I can remember. An important part of prospecting is looking at historical records of mining activity in the area you're exploring. One day as I was reading information from the Province of British Columbia, I came across this fascinating story in the 1913 Annual Report of the Minister of Mines:

"A.L. Marsh made a fortune gold mining in Nevada in the mid 1800's. But then he lost it all in a business venture in San Francisco. He headed north looking for more gold and found himself in Monashee, British Columbia. He staked a claim and began digging for bedrock, convinced that if he reached bedrock he would find another fortune. He was unable to gain financial backing, and he couldn't afford to hire anyone, so in 1889 he began digging, by himself. He tunneled 150 feet under a slide area. Then another 175 feet through blue clay. But that was just the start. He kept going—a further 2200 feet through a mix of clay, coarse gravel and boulders. For 12 years he persevered in his dream, hauling every bit of loosened ground all the way back to the surface. But then the original timber bracing he had installed more than a decade earlier began to rot and fall in. And so, still not on bedrock, Mr. Marsh had to abandon his efforts. Right up to the time of his death he continued to have "unbounded faith in the ground" though he himself was no longer young enough or strong enough to continue the rigorous work."[17]

Some might have called him foolish, or greedy, or accused him of having "gold fever"—and maybe he did—but for me, Mr. Marsh is a powerful example of perseverance. I've seen much smaller tunnels in the hills around my home where prospectors followed underground watercourses into the slopes looking for placer gold, and I can't imagine doing what they did with hand tools, much less doing what Mr. Marsh did for more than a decade. He had a dream, he had a goal, so he kept going. Rightly or wrongly, he reminds me of some of the faith heroes of Hebrews 11 who didn't ever see what

---

17 *Annual Report of the Ministry of Mines* for the Year Ending 31st December, 1913, Being an account of Mining Operations for Gold, Coal, ETC, in the Province of British Columbia

they were longing for, yet kept going. As Jesus said, *"...blessed are those who have not seen and yet have believed."* (John 20.29)

What about you? Maybe you've already quit in some way and need to get back on track. Maybe you need to start the race over, reengage as a follower of Jesus.

> *"...we are more than conquerors through him who loved us. For I am convinced that neither death nor life, neither angels nor demons, neither the present nor the future, nor any powers, neither height nor depth, nor anything else in all creation, will be able to separate us from the love of God that is in Christ Jesus our Lord." (Romans 8.37-39)*

And again from 2 Corinthians:

> *"We often suffer but we are never crushed. Even when we don't know what to do we never give up. In times of trouble God is with us, and when we are knocked down, we get up again." (2 Corinthians 4.8-9)*[18]

When we're knocked down—because of his grace, because of his presence, because of his promises, because of his help—we get up again. So persevere, with courage and peace, holding onto the Lord, resting in the fact that he is holding on to you.

A Christ Follower is persevering—throwing off excess baggage, fixing their eyes on Jesus, and resting in the hands of the Father.

---

18 Contemporary English Version® Copyright © 1995 American Bible Society. All rights reserved.

CHAPTER 9

God-Dependent

"I am the vine, you are the branches…apart from me
you can do nothing."-Jesus in John 15.5

The gun went off, we dug in, yet somehow we got off to a bad start. Two weeks earlier we'd won our class at the national championships in long-distance canoe racing, but today we found ourselves fighting from the middle of the pack of roughly 100 canoes in the largest race in North America. When that many canoes take off together, surprisingly large waves are formed. If you can get in front of the wave, you can basically surf, paddling only to keep straight, sometimes for hundreds of yards. But if you get behind such a wave, which can be three or four feet high, your only hope is to wait until the canoes spread out and the wave dissipates. At one point there was so much turbulence created by the racers fighting to get a good position that the water in front of us disappeared. We found ourselves beached, and had to jump out of our boat and run straight sideways to get back into the river.

Due to the poor start we knew we had to hit it hard to get back into the lead pack where we felt we belonged. For four hours we paddled at just slightly less than a sprint, which for us was over 70 strokes per minute, passing team after team. We were making up a lot of time; if only we could maintain the pace we would have a chance at finishing this first six-hour plus day in a good position, with two more days to make up even more time.

But then something went wrong. My heart started racing. A wave of fatigue washed over me. I could feel my heart pounding, and when I did a quick check on my pulse the rate was too high for me to count. I stopped paddling, explained to my partner Dan what was happening, and tried to catch my breath. But the expected recovery never came and I decided reluctantly that we had to pull out of the race.

Upon arriving home a week later, I was referred to a couple of heart specialists, who put me through a gamut of tests, concluding that despite my peak condition, I had what could best be described as "an electrical problem" in my heart. A twenty-four hour monitor recorded my heart beat ranging between 15 and 300 beats per minute—either of which should have knocked me flat. I was given assorted medications—one to keep my heart from beating too quickly, another to keep it from beating too slowly and a third to keep the beat regular, since it was also discovered I was experiencing occasional double beats followed by a lengthy pause. One doctor referred to it as a "fitness-induced heart problem," which still sounds ironic to me.

This all happened when I was just eighteen years old. And the jolt to my identity, my ego and my macho, teenaged sense of immortality and invincibility was both traumatic and life changing. I have some peers today, decades older than I was at the time, who have yet to figure out that their time on earth is limited, that their options are limited, and that life is indeed short. But for me, that new perspective took root just weeks after being recognized as one of the elite in my chosen sport. And it cleared the way for me to begin to embrace this next quality of a Christ Follower.

Here are some key passages that speak of this trait:

> "But he said to me, 'My grace is sufficient for you, for my power is made perfect in weakness.' Therefore I will boast all the more gladly about my weaknesses, so that Christ's power may rest on me. That is why, for Christ's sake, I delight in weaknesses, in insults, in

hardships, in persecutions, in difficulties. For when I
am weak, then I am strong." (2 Corinthians 12.9-10)

"I have been crucified with Christ and I no longer live,
but Christ lives in me. The life I now live in the body,
I live by faith in the Son of God, who loved me and
gave himself for me." (Galatians 2.20)

"I can do all this through him who gives me strength."
(Philippians 4.13)

There is also the story of Gideon in Judges 7, where Gideon and
his Israelite troops are lining up for battle against the Midianites.
The Lord tells Gideon that he has too many men. God wanted it to
be clear that it was he, not their own efforts and strength, who had
saved them. So he whittled Gideon's army down to 300 men, and
with that tiny group routed the enemy.

In contrast to our natural desire for self-sufficiency, our quest
for independence, immortality, self-made greatness—financial or
otherwise—these passages speak of a reliance on someone other
than ourselves, they call us to a posture of dependence that we are
often reluctant to admit we need. They bump us toward one aspect
of a right relationship to our Creator, which I like to refer to as
"God-Dependence."

A follower of Jesus Christ is someone who, in addition to being a
lover of God, a lover of people, holy, truth-based, evangelistic and
persevering, experiences a deep seated God-dependence. A follower
of Jesus Christ is God-dependent.

When you read through both the Old and New Testaments, this
character trait quickly becomes evident in the lives of those we
ought to emulate. It shows up in the life of Jesus, is woven throughout the record of the early church in Acts and the letters, and is
even hinted at in the last verse of the Bible.

And yet this essential trait flies in the face of our natural bent.
We work hard to achieve "financial independence" and the resulting freedom from the bank, a regular paycheck, the government.

God-Dependent   125

Self-sufficiency appeals to us, whether it shows up in the ability to tell our boss to "take this job and shove it," to fix our own lawn-mower, to sew our own clothes or to heat our houses with wood we've cut ourselves.

A lot of the appeal of the Y2K rush at the start of the new millennium was that it gave people an opportunity to become more independent—whether through a massive stockpile of food, the ability to generate their own power, or the knowledge and resources to survive, even thrive, without government services, at least for a time. And on one level this desire isn't wrong at all.

> "Yet we urge you, dear friends, to do so more and more, and to make it your ambition to lead a quiet life: You should mind your own business and work with your hands, just as we told you, so that your daily life may win the respect of outsiders and so that you will not be dependent on anybody." (I Thessalonians 4.10-12)

A certain amount of independence is okay, commendable, a worthy goal. But this is the wrong posture when it comes to our relationship with God.

Foundational Attitudes of God Dependence

I shared earlier, in the evangelistic chapter, the story of Grant, the first person I had the privilege of sharing the basic Gospel with and seeing a solid crossing-the-line response. He was so aware of his need for God, for forgiveness, for a Saviour, that he interrupted my memorized explanation of "the bad news" so he could more quickly hear about the solution to his sin.

In contrast to that exchange with Grant is a far more common experience I have in sharing Christ with "more respectable" people. Their response to the bad news usually goes something like this: "Well, yes I have done a few wrong things, but who hasn't? I'm not really a bad person. I know people who go to church who are far worse than me! And to say that I deserve death for what I have done, that I deserve hell, come on, I'm not Hitler, I'm not Saddam, I'm not a serial killer, I'm not _____." (Insert the name of our culture's current personification of evil.)

Are people in single-family suburban dwellings less sinful than those in the inner city? Are middle-class people more righteous than lower-class people or the upper-class one percent? Not a chance. There is simply more self-righteousness and pride in some people than in others. Yes, there are self-righteous inner city people, just as there are many very well off people who admit freely that they are, like everyone else, dirty rotten sinners. But it seems that the foundational attitude of humility comes easier to people in humble circumstances, to people whose brokenness isn't hidden by a façade of manicured lawns, fashionable clothes and nice cars.

Behind the character quality of God-dependence is the foundational attitude of humility.

In both the Old and New Testaments of the Bible we read that "God opposes the proud but gives grace to the humble." This truth is illustrated again and again throughout scripture. What does it mean that God opposes the proud, that he gives grace to the humble? It means that God doesn't help those who don't think they need help. At the same time, he is completely available to those who are desperate. Proud people act as if they are independent of God, and perhaps actually believe they are. But humble people know they need God. They confess it freely, they even embrace it. Jesus said he didn't come to call the righteous but to call sinners to repentance, that it is the sick (i.e., those who know they are "sick") not the well (the independent and self-sufficient), who need a doctor.

Do you need God? Yes, you do. But do you know you need God? Not just for salvation, but also for day to day life? A Christ Follower has woven into their DNA the knowledge, the conviction that says, "I need God…desperately."

In addition to humility, there is a second foundational attitude associated with God-dependence, highlighted in this passage:

*"And without faith it is impossible to please God,
because anyone who comes to him must believe that
he exists and that he rewards those who earnestly seek
him." (Hebrews 11.6)*

Along with humility, a foundational attitude (or perhaps posture) is faith.

While humility says, "I need God..." faith adds, "...he can and will help me." Christ Followers both know they need God (humility) and that God can and will help them (faith).

One day while Jesus was teaching, he spoke his famous lines, "Ask and it will be given to you..." But then he asked a question: "Dads, if you have a son who wants some bread, are you going to give him a stone?"

Think about that for a moment. Perhaps you are a parent. If not, think of someone you love deeply. Your child, or that person you love so much, is hungry. And you grab a rock from the side of the street and say, "Here, eat this." But it's a rock! "Yes, but it's kind of shiny, nice and round...mmm mmm. "

Ridiculous picture isn't it? In that same exchange Jesus also asked, "If your son asks for a fish to eat, are you going to give him a snake?" The answer to each question is obvious, rhetorical: "No, of course not!" Then Jesus says:

*"If you, then, though you are evil, know how to give
good gifts to your children, how much more will your
Father in heaven give good gifts to those who ask him!"*
(Matthew 7.11)

Faith is an expectation that God will act in keeping with his character and his Word, that he is attentive to the cries of his children, and able to do something about our greatest needs.

Do you know you need God, no matter how together your life seems to be? Do you know God can and will help you, no matter how messed up your life seems to be? Humility and faith, being able to say, "I need God and he can and will help me," is foundational to the character quality of God-dependence.

Now, where there is a deep-rooted faith and humility, there is bound to be a visible response, there will be some accompanying action. God-dependence is founded on humility and faith, and it results in some specific actions.

Foundational Actions of God Dependence

If you, on one hand, know you need God, and, on the other hand believe that he can and will help you, what will you do when you are in need—whether casual need or crisis? You will ask for his help. You will pray. Which means that when we are in need (as we always are on some scale) and we don't pray, it is likely due to an absence of our awareness of need, or a lack of understanding or faith in his willingness and ability to meet that need.

One of the actions arising from the conviction that "I need God and he can and will help me" is prayer.

I used to pray because I thought I had to pray as a duty, because that's what Christians do. In fact, at one point in my life I made a deal with God (ever done that?) to read one chapter of the Bible and pray for five minutes every day, if he would do what I was asking. I would quickly plow through a chapter, then pull out my stopwatch and pray for exactly five minutes, no more, no less. Surprisingly, the Lord used that small opening, tainted motives and all, to get a deep hold of my heart.

In time I discovered that I actually needed the Lord's hand in my life—not simply to fulfill my selfish whims, but to give me meaning and purpose and direction and true success in light of eternity. And I discovered that the way my many great needs get connected to God's resources is through faith, showing up in prayer. So I no longer pray because I'm supposed to pray. I pray because I need to pray, I pray because I need God to intervene in my life, to break through my stubbornness, my self-centeredness, my weakness, my fear. I pray because I need God. And I have discovered that the Word is true—he is both willing and able to help me. He calls me, and you, to "Ask, Seek, Knock."

When I look at the struggles and guilt many individuals and churches face regarding their lack of prayer, I can't help but wonder if it's due to an absence of conscious God-dependence. And perhaps accompanying that absence of God-dependence is a low-risk life-style or ministry where we are not attempting anything that requires the Lord to show up.

Prayer is not merely a duty, a task—though it can indeed be work when we get into deep warfare and intercession. Rather, prayer is a privilege. Prayer is an opportunity to open the doors of our lives, the lives of others, and all kinds of impossible situations to the power of the Almighty God.

Do you have an impossible situation in your life? Are you under the weather or over your head in some way? You need God. God can and will help you. And if you believe that, you will jump at the opportunity to call out to him for help. You will pray. It goes hand-in-hand with God-dependence.

> "They devoted themselves to the apostles' teaching and
> to fellowship, to the breaking of bread and to prayer."
> (Acts 2.42)

Why did prayer so thoroughly permeate the early church? It was because these followers of Jesus were desperate. They knew, on the one hand, how needy they were and, on the other hand, how willing and able God was to meet them at their point of need. Jesus had modeled the pattern of daily desperation for the Father before his disciples, and they knew that they likewise needed to come before God for direction, strength, and other resources. That knowledge seems to be a prerequisite for God-dependence and the resulting move to prayer.

There are several other actions or postures that show up in some-one who is God-dependent:

- Gratitude. When we know that all we have comes from God, we are grateful.
- Reliance on the Holy Spirit. Again we have the example of the early Christians who waited in Jerusalem until they were "clothed with power from on high," and constantly relied on the Spirit's leading and empowering.
- Peace. The Bible talks about the peace that transcends all understanding—a peace that makes no sense based on circumstances. If you've ever snorkeled or scuba-dived in rough water you know the amazing transformation that takes place the moment you drop beneath the surface. Turbulence becomes peace. This is not unlike the peace that comes from knowing you need God, knowing he can and will help you, calling out to him in prayer, and waiting in expectation for his answer.
- Boldness. In Acts 4, the disciples were threatened and told to talk no more about Jesus. They said, "You've gotta be kidding!? If you'd seen what we've seen you'd know why we can't shut up!" (Loose paraphrase.) After their release they gathered in prayer. *"After they prayed, the place where they were meeting was shaken. And they were all filled with the Holy Spirit and spoke the word of God boldly."* (Acts 4.31)
- God-dependence springs from a foundation of humility and faith, and results in prayer, gratitude, reliance on the Spirit, peace and boldness.

Three weeks into my first pastorate I thought I was going to die. I was, and am, an introvert. Only a couple months before, in my final semester of Bible college, I was still so shy that I had difficulty raising my hand in class to ask a question. And now I was leading a church. I enjoyed the time to study the Word, I enjoyed ministry planning, even one on one meeting with leaders. But every Sunday I had to get up in front of the church and speak. Everyone was looking at me and they expected me to say something profound. And it was killing me. Following that third Sunday morning service of what felt like a slow, torturous asphyxiation, I got alone in my office and with my face to the floor cried out for help. I said, "Lord, I know you've called me to be a pastor. Not only that, I know you have called me here. But I can't do it. I need you to do something or I think I will die from the sheer stress of having to preach."

I was unaware of any change until I got up to speak the next week. To my surprise, I enjoyed it. It still tired me out, I still had a certain level of nervous tension prior to the message, but it was an entirely different experience. I'd received his strength for my weakness. To this day I look back at those messages with gratitude and amazement, both at the content and the results in people's lives. I knew I couldn't do it; but I knew enough to know that he equips us for what he calls us to. Even today, when I get up to preach, regardless of whether the message is "good" or "bad," the simple fact that I am speaking in public is, for me, proof of God's faithfulness and his power.

I have had many opportunities, both in pastoral ministry and my personal life, to repeat that process again and again. With great frequency I come up against something I know I am supposed to do, while at the same time knowing I am incapable. But I know the Lord can and will help me, and he does. And I've learned that, like those first believers in the book of Acts, a cry for help is often better done in the context of a group rather than solo. All of these character traits, while individual, are best nurtured in community.

Disciples of Jesus Christ are God-dependent. They know they are desperately needy. But that does not lead to despair because they also know their God can and will help them. He created them, us, to need him. Can you affirm from the bottom of your heart that no matter how good things might be going at the moment, "I need God?" Can you say, perhaps in the midst of things much bigger than you, impossible situations, "God can and will help me?" That's what it means to be God-dependent. And God dependence is an essential part of what it means to be a Christ Follower.

A Christ Follower is God-Dependent, someone who knows they desperately need God, and that God can and will help them. So they cry out to him from a posture of humility and faith, and find that he is sufficient for all their needs.

CHAPTER 10

Focused on Eternity

*"But our citizenship is in heaven. And we eagerly
await a Savior from there, the Lord Jesus Christ..."*
(Philippians 3.20)

The 2002 Australian film *Rabbit Proof Fence* tells the true story
of three aboriginal girls removed from their home and family
in Jigalong, Western Australia, in 1931. Sisters Molly and Daisy,
along with their cousin Gracie, were "half-castes," children of white
fathers and aboriginal mothers. The Aborigine Act of the day allowed children from anywhere in the state to be placed in residen-
tial schools. The fairer-skinned ones were educated and married off
to white husbands. The grandchildren of these unions were seen as
white, eliminating this unwanted third race.

In the film, the three girls are literally ripped from their mother
and grandmother's arms and transported by truck and train, sometimes caged, to the school at Moore River. Here they are placed in a
dorm with dozens of other half-caste girls, and begin to experience
the regimented prison-like conditions of the school. Those who try
to escape are caught by the aboriginal tracker Moodoo and pun-
ished severely.

One day, with a storm on the horizon, Molly decides to run away
with her sister and cousin, hoping that the rain will obscure their
tracks. This begins an amazing trek in which the girls attempt to
evade capture and find the resources and directions they need to get

home. A key to their success is the rabbit-proof fence, a 1500-mile structure, the longest fence in the world, built to keep the plague of introduced rabbits contained and separated from the good farmland. One line of the fence runs right thru Jigalong, the girls' home. Upon finding the fence they follow it doggedly, continuing to elude the tracker, police and others who have been enlisted to catch them. At one point Gracie is captured and returned to Moore River. The two sisters continue on for several more weeks, through desolate wilderness and into a desert where they nearly perish. Finally, by following the fence, they are joyfully reunited with their mother and grandmother, who take them to hide in the desert.

To get home, the girls walked for nine weeks and covered about 1200 miles. Incredibly, Molly was later taken to Moore River with her own children, escaped, and made the same journey home carrying a baby. The movie closes with a shot of Daisy and Molly, now very old women, still at Jigalong, vowing never to leave home again.[19]

So far we have seen that a follower of Jesus Christ is A Lover of God, A Lover of People, Holy, Truth-Based, Evangelistic, Persevering and God-Dependent.

The final non-negotiable character trait of a follower of Jesus Christ reflects the craving God has put in our hearts for our true home: A follower of Jesus Christ is focused on eternity. The longing of Molly and Daisy to get home, along with the challenges and setbacks and difficulties they faced, is a vivid picture of a longing we all have: The longing to arrive at the place of complete wholeness and unhindered fellowship with our Creator; to experience and witness the resurrection and renewal of all things; to finally taste the state of perfection for which we were made.

> "Therefore we do not lose heart. Though outwardly we
> are wasting away, yet inwardly we are being renewed
> day by day. For our light and momentary troubles are
> achieving for us an eternal glory that far outweighs

---

19 *Rabbit Proof Fence.* Hanway Films. 2002. DVD

them all. So we fix our eyes not on what is seen, but on what is unseen, since what is seen is temporary, but what is unseen is eternal." (2 Corinthians 4.16-18)

"Since, then, you have been raised with Christ, set your hearts on things above, where Christ is, seated at the right hand of God. Set your minds on things above, not on earthly things. For you died, and your life is now hidden with Christ in God. When Christ, who is your life, appears, then you also will appear with him in glory." (Colossians 3.1-4)

Followers of Jesus Christ are focused on eternity. This means that even though we are in the here and now, our hearts are longing for what is yet to come. This trait intersects with the other character qualities we've explored. In fact, many of them make no sense apart from eternity:

- When we see what God has prepared for us we love him more.
- When we see how much God loves his creation, and understand his desire and plan to restore it, we are motivated to love people more and gain a greater sense of our responsibility as stewards of creation.
- The imminent arrival of eternity stirs us to be holy. *"All who have this hope in him purify themselves, just as he is pure."* (1 John 3.3)
- The prospect of eternity drives us to the Word, pushes us to be more renewed in our thinking and our priorities so that we are prepared for *"the life that is truly life."* (1 Timothy 6.19).
- The reality of eternity, combined with the knowledge that everyone will live forever somewhere, in some state of restored or permanently broken relationship with their Creator, is a massive motivation for evangelism.

- When we know what's coming, both the challenges and the rewards, we are enabled to persevere.
- When we realize that eternity is a gift from our Creator, and that he sees the beginning from the end, it moves us back to a place of dependence on him for the here and now.

One person's definition of a Christian is someone who looks like a fool until Jesus shows up. And there is some truth in that. A follower of Jesus, focused on eternity, won't always make sense within our present framework of time and space on earth. To be focused on eternity means that while we exist in the here and now, our hearts are longing for what is yet to come, groaning with all creation for the ultimate and final liberation. It means that as fully engaged as we may be in this life, as much as we may enjoy it, we know there is something more, something greater, and we live for that time, that place, that state.

[Note: There are subtle and some not-so-subtle differences and overlapping ideas in the various understandings and convictions regarding the final state: Intermediate heaven vs ultimate heaven vs the millennium vs the Kingdom vs new heaven and new earth vs eternity. For this reason I am primarily using the word "eternity" as a summary statement for our final time/space destination as followers of Jesus Christ and for the era following the resurrection and renewal of all things. I may at times use it to refer to the believer's immediate post-death experience, well aware that this is distinct from the final state, since at that point the individual has, in some measure, entered eternity. Further, though I fully accept the biblical testimony regarding the final state of people who have not been redeemed, often summarized by the word "hell," I am not focusing here on that very real aspect of eternity since it is not related to the character traits being addressed. Likewise, the few times I use heaven, unless otherwise stated, I am using it in this same sense of our, and creation's, final renewed time/space state.]

Those Focused on Eternity Prepare for Eternity

People who are focused on eternity are not passive, they are not killing time until time is gone, they are actively preparing for eternity. In Matthew 6, Jesus talks about storing up treasures in heaven. In 1 Timothy, Paul talks about using our money to lay up treasure as a firm foundation for the coming age. Someone with an eternal perspective, someone who is focused on eternity, will think and talk and live far differently than someone whose primary motivation is squeezing as much pleasure as possible out of the here and now. If someone is focused on eternity, they may look like they are fully engaged in the here and now, but like all creation they are longing for what is to come, and this affects both what they do and why they do what they do now.

Many years ago I came across this story in a farming journal:

"In olden times kings often had a court jester, sometimes called a court fool, who amused the royal court with humorous antics. One day a king gave his scepter to his court fool saying, 'Go throughout my kingdom, and if you find a greater fool than yourself, give him this scepter.'

After a long time the fool returned, and found the king very sick, near death. 'I am going on a long journey and I will not return,' said the king. 'And how long have you known you would have to make this journey,' asked the fool. 'For a long time,' said the king. 'And what preparation have you made for this long journey?' asked the fool. 'I am afraid I have never made any preparation,' said the king, 'and I am not ready to go.'

'Here is your scepter,' said the fool, 'You are a bigger fool than I am.'"[20]

---

20 *Alberta Farm Life*, November 7, 1994

There are many obstacles to a life focused on eternity, to a life that actively prepares for eternity. Eternity is often overshadowed by the rush and challenges and pleasures of the here and now. Karl Marx called religion "the opium of the people," something that makes us put up with oppression and suffering because we are holding a hope for the future, and we think, wrongly, that something better is coming. Even as Christ Followers, we often fear drifting into a state of being "too heavenly minded to be any earthly good"— as if that were possible. In reality, a focus on eternity gives us the right perspective, the right priorities for the present. In a way, Marx was right. The idea of heaven can help in times of suffering. But what if it is not, as he thought, just a psychological drug? What if this isn't all there is?

> "We are very shy nowadays of even mentioning heaven. We are afraid of the jeer about 'pie in the sky,' and of being told that we are trying to 'escape' from the duty of making a happy world here and now into dreams of a happy world elsewhere. But either there is 'pie in the sky' or there is not. If there is not, then Christianity is false, for this doctrine is woven into its whole fabric. If there is, then this truth, like any other, must be faced…"[21]

Followers of Jesus Christ who accept the Bible as God's word, who accept the teaching of the Lord himself as truth, cannot avoid the emphasis on eternity, the assumption that eternal values must be used to interpret our present-day activities and ambitions. So, the obvious questions are, "How do we gain and develop and keep that focus on eternity?" and "How can we be captured by an eternal perspective that impacts every facet of our lives?"

When I look at the list of the eight character qualities I believe are essential for Christ Followers, there are some that occasionally make me cringe. They reveal just how far I have to go. But there are other traits that somehow by the grace of God have become

---

21 C.S. Lewis, *The Problem of Pain*, © C.S. Lewis Pte Ltd 1940, 115

locked into the core of my being. This focus on eternity has shaped me immensely.

I think about eternity a lot. The powerful song by Mercy Me, *I Can Only Imagine*, moves me to tears almost every time I listen to it. Perhaps it's partly due to my work as a pastor over the years, dealing with people in seasons of great loss. Maybe it's because what I am giving my life to only makes sense in light of eternity. But I think it's more than that. I love life, I enjoy so much on this earth. I've had the privilege of living in some of the most beautiful places in the world. I've had a very full and interesting life. I like it here right now! But I would let it all go in a moment for eternity.

I want eternity: I want to see my dad who died on Christmas Eve, 1994; I look forward to seeing my grandmother who wrote letters to me as a child and who once wrote me a letter and then died before I replied. I want time to end, and eternity to start so that true justice can be ushered in and the mind-numbing suffering happening right now, as it has for centuries around the world, can be stopped. I want to be done with the battle against sin and the flesh and Satan. I want to see people's minds and bodies fixed at the resurrection in a way they will never be fixed here and now, even with the greatest medical advances. I want to see the new heaven and the new earth, the restoration of creation. I want his kingdom to come and his will to be done on earth as it is in heaven. I want to see every knee bow and every tongue confess that Jesus Christ is Lord to the glory of God the Father. I want to see Jesus and say, "Thank You." I want to explore all there will be to explore for all eternity. It is going to be… great? Awesome? Spectacular? Overwhelmingly good? Words are inadequate. "No eye has seen, no ear has heard, no mind has conceived…" I believe that the only thing in my existence that matters is getting there and bringing as many with me as possible.

Those Focused on Eternity Reflect on Eternity

So again, how do we gain that eternal perspective? How does a focus on eternity become woven into our souls? As simple as it sounds, I believe a significant part of the answer is this: We get an eternal perspective by thinking about eternity. Yes, by thinking about it, mulling on it, reflecting on its reality. So let's think about eternity for a few minutes.

I used to believe that the most important thing I could accomplish with a sermon or a piece of writing was getting people to go DO something. And that's important. Truth leads to action. Faith without works is dead. But what really seems to change us is when we think deeply about something, when we let biblical truth ooze into our pores and immerse us in its power. Thinking and reflecting on the big ideas of scripture are among the most difficult things to do, but they are also among the highest-leverage, most life-changing things we can do. So let's think about eternity for a bit.

Do you have any idea what eternity means? The Bible uses the phrase "forever and ever" in several places. How long is that? I like this description of eternity:

> "High up in the North, the land called Svithjod, there stands a rock. It is 100 miles high and 100 miles wide. Once every 1000 years a little bird comes to this rock to sharpen its beak. When the rock has thus been worn away, then a single day of eternity will have gone by."[22]

Think about how long eternity is. It is mind numbing. We can't grasp it. It makes this life look like a spark that flashes for a fraction of a second and then disappears forever.

The website deathclock.com describes itself as "the internet's friendly reminder that life is slipping away." You go to the site and enter your date of birth, your gender, whether you are normal, optimistic, pessimistic or sadistic. You also state whether or not you are a smoker, and can also add your BMI (body mass index). When you click, "Check Your Death Clock" it does a calculation based on statistics and life expectancies to tell you when you will likely die. A box with a large number comes up, the number of seconds you have

---

22 From *The Story of Mankind* by Hendrik Willem Van Loon, 1921

left to live, and as you watch, the number is counting down second by second. It can be a little shocking for some people. If you have already lived past the average life expectancy, a message comes up that says "I am sorry. Your time has expired. Have a nice day."

Regardless of how accurate deathclock.com is, or by how much you beat the average life expectancy, the clock really is ticking for all of us. And at one point our time will have expired and we will enter eternity. It is a certainty. This life will end and eternity will begin. Becoming convinced of our own mortality is an important part of becoming focused on eternity.

I had a friend named Dave who, like me, was in his early 40s at the time, and whose children were the same ages as mine. So when he was diagnosed with ALS, Lou Gehrig's disease, it struck very close to home. Over the following three years as his condition deteriorated and he was eventually placed in a care home, slowly losing the ability to walk, feed himself, and speak, he became captivated by heaven, by eternity. He was greatly encouraged by Randy Alcorn's book Heaven and gave away the short booklet version to many. (As an aside, Randy Alcorn's ministry is called Eternal Perspective Ministries. And that's just what his writing gives you. So if you need to grow in your focus on eternity, next to the Bible, I'd suggest you find some of Randy's work.)

One day I was visiting with Dave—he was still able to speak though with difficulty—and we talked about the many prayers going up for his healing. He said, "You know, I'd like to be healed. God would definitely get the glory because we know the doctors can't do anything. But you know, the more I read about heaven, the more I think about it, I'm not too sure I want to be healed. I'm really looking forward to heaven." And then he said something that became his refrain in his final days, "Healing or Heaven, I can't lose, it's a win-win!"

A few weeks before his death, in an email exchange made possible by a technology that allowed Dave to type with his eyes, he replied to one of my observations from scripture with this statement:

"I am learning by force that doing nothing, but trusting and believing, is more peacefully fruitful than we can imagine."

How was that kind of grace, dignity, hope and peace possible, even when everything else was stripped away? It was possible because Dave had an unwavering focus on eternity. A short time after our exchange he got his "Well done!"

Joni Eareckson Tada, paralyzed since her teen years, has made some profound statements about heaven and eternity in her teachings. Among my favorites is this quote:

> "I have hope in the future. The Bible speaks about bodies
> being glorified. I know the meaning of that now. It's the time
> after my death here, when I, the quadriplegic, will be on my
> feet dancing."[23]

The movie Amistad is a powerful true story based on the plight of a group of Africans captured to be sold as slaves. They take over the ship they are being transported on but then are arrested, held in prison and tried for piracy and murder. While they are being held in prison, one of them named Yamba is given a Bible. One day he is flipping through it looking at the pictures since he couldn't read the English. A man named Cinque, the leader and spokesman of the slaves, begins talking with him, and Yamba walks his friend through the story of the Bible, including the life, death and resurrection of Jesus, culminating with a scene of heaven. He says "This is where we are going when they kill us." And after a pause concludes, "It doesn't look so bad."[24]

Could you find comfort in the reality of heaven while sitting in a dark, damp cell awaiting a trial in which you will likely be found guilty and executed, even though you are innocent? How strong is your "focus on eternity"?

---

23 quoted by John R. W. Stott in his sermon The Up-to-the-Minute Relevance of the Resurrection. Preaching Today, Tape 79
24 Amistad. Dreamworks. 1997. DVD.

"Then I saw 'a new heaven and a new earth,' for the first heaven and the first earth had passed away, and there was no longer any sea. I saw the Holy City, the new Jerusalem, coming down out of heaven from God, prepared as a bride beautifully dressed for her husband. And I heard a loud voice from the throne saying, 'Look! God's dwelling place is now among the people, and he will dwell with them. They will be his people, and God himself will be with them and be their God. 'He will wipe every tear from their eyes. There will be no more death' or mourning or crying or pain, for the old order of things has passed away.' He who was seated on the throne said, 'I am making everything new!' Then he said, 'Write this down, for these words are trustworthy and true.'" (Revelation 21.1-5)

As C.S. Lewis stated, "All that is not eternal is eternally out of date."

When Jesus gave his disciples the Lord's supper, a symbol of his suffering and death, he told them to repeat the ceremony until he returned. With this directive Jesus was building right into the fabric of the worship of the church a reminder not just of his death, but of his return, of the end of the age, of eternity. For apart from eternity, what sense would his sacrifice make?

I have found that stories, quotes and ideas like the ones shared in this chapter stir me to think about eternity. They move me, and hopefully you, to what I believe is a "sanctified daydreaming," where we become captivated by the promises of the Lord for creation's eternal destination, our eternal state of freedom and the accompanying unbroken relationships, joy and satisfaction—forever.

Sometimes when we focus on eternity we just want to go home. The journey isn't always easy. Yet we know that because of Jesus, our ultimate arrival at our true home is assured. "And so we will be with the Lord forever." (1 Thessalonians 4.17) Until then, we are called to enjoy life, work hard, relax in the warm sun or in a cool body of water, bask in the beauty of creation while at the same time keeping our eyes above the horizon, keeping our focus on eternity.

There once was a man who endured great suffering. He had every reason to give up, to quit, to lose faith. But instead, this man Job said:

> "I know that my redeemer lives, and that in the end he will stand on the earth. And after my skin has been destroyed, yet in my flesh I will see God; I will see him with my own eyes—I, and not another. How my heart yearns within me!" (Job 19.25-27)

A disciple of Jesus Christ is many things, has many character qualities woven into their spiritual DNA. And among the most important is this focus on eternity.

———•—•———

A Christ Follower is focused on eternity, engaged in the here and now but longing for what is yet to come.

———•—•———

Section III

The Church's Challenge

A Church That
Makes Christ Followers

*"Come follow me," Jesus said, "and I will send you out
to fish for people." (Matthew 4.19)*

Have you ever heard of whirling disease? Back in the 1950s fish shipments from Europe accidentally transmitted the parasite myxobulus cerebralis into North American waters. The parasite is carried by a certain kind of worm, and when it is eaten by a trout or a salmon, the parasite damages the cartilage around the fish's brain. This results in head or skeletal deformities that cause the creatures to lose their balance, so they spin or corkscrew in the water until they die. Hence the name whirling disease. While this problem could potentially destroy an outstanding sport fishery, biologists tell us that the parasite does not affect humans. So there must be another reason why so many churches seem to be spinning in circles.

I am a product of the North American evangelical church. My family was one of three families to start a church in our community in my early teen years. This was the church I was baptized in, the church I grew up in. I'm grateful for my heritage, and have benefited from the teaching, encouragement, and relationships I've experienced over the years. When I was fourteen I was given the chance to preach my first sermon, which, due to my rapid rate of speech, turned out to be an epic five-minute sprint through Romans

14, but which, due to the encouragement of my pastor, planted the seeds of future ministry. And I will never forget the exceptional care this body of believers provided for my family, especially my mother, when my father passed away from cancer at the age of fifty-four. They were the hands and feet of Christ, and in that season gave me a snapshot of how the church can provide a level of care and service, true community, that no secular organization rivals.

I'm grateful to the many who have worked and are working so hard to make the church a better representation of the Lord's intent, despite incredible opposition from the critics. "Thank You" to Willow Creek, Saddleback, North Point, Christ the Saviour and the men and women in the trenches in these and other ministries. Thank you to the many denominational leaders who take on the daunting task of overseeing dozens, hundreds, thousands of churches and their pastors. I'm indebted to the simple church pioneers who seek to boil church down to its biblical and practical essence. And finally, I'm especially thankful for the women and men, who through the centuries to the present time, have challenged us to pray, seek revival, pursue a deeper work of the Holy Spirit, and immerse ourselves in the Word.

For more than twenty years I've been a pastor. I've served in denominational roles, been to dozens of conferences and retreats, read the books, scanned the websites. In recent years, in my role as a transitional pastor I have seen many churches in crisis. I know the good and the bad of the church from the inside. Occasionally, when someone is complaining about a church or the Church, I feel like jumping in and saying, "Oh, it's far worse than that!" Yet on the other hand, when someone is highlighting one of the ways a church or the Church has gotten it right, I want to interrupt and say, "Oh, it is far better than that!"

I wouldn't describe my attitude toward the church as 'love-hate'; I think it's more accurate to call it a 'love but often frustrated to the point of tears' relationship. And I've discovered I am not alone. Some suggest that the fastest growing segment of Christianity in North America consists of those who consider themselves Christians, but are no longer attached to any church. Regardless of the actual hard data, I've seen that a significant number of these are former pastors and church workers.

What are We Measuring?

One of the reasons for this exodus is a ridiculous ever-changing pastoral workload brought on by the moving target of 'what the people want.' This is influenced by the accessibility of diverse Christian teachers and teaching from around the world, as well as an increasingly a-la-carte larger culture. It seems that we lack a focus, and perhaps at times the courage, to say as leaders and churches, "This is what we are called to be and do. Let's figure out together how to do it here."

> "Then Jesus came to them and said, 'All authority in heaven and on earth has been given to me. Therefore go and make disciples of all nations, baptizing them in the name of the Father and of the Son and of the Holy Spirit, and teaching them to obey everything I have commanded you. And surely I am with you always, to the very end of the age.'" (Matthew 28.18-20)

I'm going to forego the long discussion of all the possible end goals for the church, and simply state what I think is obvious. I believe that the bottom line, end target for the church, and for individual disciples of Jesus Christ, is making disciples. I believe that the purpose of every biblical church, regardless of the exact details in the wording—turning irreligious people into fully devoted followers of Jesus, leading people to follow Jesus, bringing people to a radically relevant encounter with Jesus Christ, or whatever creative contextual slogan we develop—is to "make disciples." And it seems that most churches (at least evangelical churches) and Christian leaders agree with this. My own tribe, the Christian & Missionary Alliance in Canada, puts it this way in our Local Church Constitution:

The purpose of this church is to glorify God by proclaiming the good news of Jesus Christ and persuading men and women to become his disciples and dependable members of his Church.[25]

Despite the seeming unanimity around the idea of making disciples, surprisingly few churches and denominations have bothered defining what they mean by "disciple" or "Christ Follower." Even fewer have focused their resources to accomplish that task in an effective, efficient and measurable way, foregoing activities that contribute little if anything to that purpose.

> *"Those who accepted his message were baptized, and about three thousand were added to their number that day." (Acts 2.41)*

> *"But many who heard the message believed; so the number of men who believed grew to about five thousand." (Acts 4.4)*

Organizational theory tells us that "what gets measured gets done." The early church actually counted baptisms, the birth of new disciples. If we're not measuring "disciple-making," in even a rudimentary way like conversions or baptism, what are we actually trying to accomplish, how do we define "success" as a church, as a group of Christ Followers in community? Every church seems to measure attendance. So...are we simply making attendees?

Shaking the Etch A Sketch®

Whenever I'm in a meeting or conversation with someone and want us to move to zero-based thinking, imagining that we are starting from scratch in addressing an issue or solving a problem, I suggest that we need to "shake the Etch A Sketch®" referring to the method of erasing doodles on the very popular (pre computer, tablet, video game console) children's toy.

---

25 *Manual of the Christian & Missionary Alliance in Canada*, 2014, 31

I believe this is how we should approach church and the personal application of our Christian beliefs, especially with regard to disciple-making.

Today we find ourselves in an odd, very inefficient, and mostly ineffective system for following Jesus together. The way we "do church" is a mish-mash of ideas developed from scripture (often with little differentiation between Old Testament and New Testament concepts), church history, popular culture and influential Christian thinkers both dead and living. And while I can't be sure of the motives of all those who have been involved in developing this system (I have a hard enough time with my own motives!), it sure looks like "making disciples" ceased to be the prime consideration at some point. When I observe the average church's activities it often seems that making disciples isn't the top priority, or even a high priority, or in some cases even a conscious priority, despite mission, vision and purpose statements to the contrary. Even having a "pastor of discipleship" is no guarantee that a church is actively producing Christ Followers, and depending on the assumptions governing such a role, may in fact be an indication that it is not. (What are the other pastors doing if not involved in making disciples??) In the rare cases where disciple-making is taken seriously, the process of making disciples is often forced into a church system which was not designed for this purpose, and which in fact has structures and systems in place that interfere with it.

"What you win them with is what you win them to." I'm not sure who said it first, but they were right. If a church is full of people who have come to that church with a consumer mindset, often from another church, because it puts on a good show (interesting, relevant preaching, inspiring worship, great children's program) and has full-service programing, the attendance numbers could mean very little. If some event like a staff change or downturn in finances removes the specific hook that brought them to the church, they may go looking elsewhere.

So let's shake the Etch-a-Sketch®.

Let's pretend there is no organized church in our city or region or even country, that there is no right or wrong way of doing things apart from biblical principles, that there are no internal special interest groups to please (yes I know—hard to imagine in a local church setting), no preconceived ideas of what the ministries and programs ought to be, just a desire to fulfil the Lord's call to be and to make disciples.

My thinking in this area is incomplete and still essentially embryonic, though not recent. I've been mulling on this issue for more than a decade. Here are some initial thoughts to toss into the stewpot of your own thinking about this challenge.

Step 1: Clearly State the Purpose

The first essential step in building a church that makes Christ Followers is to identify the target. Get very clear on why you are doing what you are doing. If you're running a marathon you want to finish in a certain place or with a certain time. If you're redecorating a home you have a certain style or atmosphere in mind. And if you are following Jesus, then you are involved in making disciples, more followers of Jesus Christ. As stated earlier, most churches and Christian leaders will agree with this end. Where we fall down is at Step 2.

Step 2: Know What the Target Looks Like

There's a joke up here in Canada about some hunters "from a country to our south," who come up moose hunting. They are successful on their first day, but they have to fight off a cowboy who is trying to take their kill. Finally the cowboy says, "Ok, I'll let you keep the meat, but can I at least remove the saddle?"

In any endeavor it's important to clearly define what the target, what success actually looks like, otherwise we are prone to redefining what we are doing as hitting the target. It's like shooting an arrow at a board and then drawing the target and bullseye around it. If we decide our purpose is making disciples, we might simply point to our current outcomes (attendance, giving, the number of people on mission trips) as evidence of success in disciple-making.

It is actually quite easy to gather a group of people we call "disciples" who in fact bear little resemblance, in character or conduct, to biblical followers of Jesus Christ.

One of the purposes of this book and the eight traits I've shared is to provide a starting point for answering the question, "What is a follower of Jesus Christ, in character?" I'm not terribly concerned if my specific conclusions are accepted as they are, modified, or jettisoned altogether. My concern and hope is simply that:

1. Church leaders and church members will agree that as a primary part of their ministry they are called to make disciples.

2. Based on that conviction they will become clear and united in their minds what a disciple looks like, what it is they are trying to (called to!) build, and then...

Step 3: Allocate Resources and Develop Ministries to Produce the Desire Results

Within a few months of my first pastorate it hit me: Church attendance and involvement, even beyond Sunday morning, was no guarantee that a Christian was growing and being developed into an effective follower of Jesus Christ. To use Sonlife terminology, there is usually a lot of Building going on in our churches, but very little Winning and Equipping. Most of our ministries and programs transmit knowledge, but not skill. Occasionally we provide some motivation, but without the ability or clear instruction on how to apply what we have stirred them to do, our people fail when it comes to application.

If we say, for instance, that a follower of Jesus Christ is evangelistic, it isn't enough to simply motivate our people for evangelism. There is also some obvious training and modelling called for, such as how to:

- Intercede for those who have yet to come to repentance and faith
- Share our personal stories and the larger Gospel story
- Help my friends who repent and believe move toward baptism and a grounding in the faith.

- Every facet of the DNA description of what a follower of Jesus Christ is in character calls for a related ministry focus (not just teaching, but often training) of some kind to help instill that trait and the related skills, attitudes, motivations, and relationships in the follower. And while some aspects of this disciple-making can happen in a large group context, some must happen in a smaller group, and others develop best in a one-on-one context.

The Prerequisite of Regeneration

A growing problem in evangelical churches, a problem that we sometimes condescendingly assume is isolated in the mainline churches, is that of attendees, members, even leaders, who have never been born again. That is, they are not "Christian" in any biblical sense of the word. A friend of mine who helps churches in crisis once went to such a church, and in his initial one-on-one meetings with the leadership, discovered a man who had been an elder in the church for more than a decade who was not a believer in Jesus Christ. Little wonder that this particular church was in crisis!

The starting point for making disciples must be repentance and faith in Jesus Christ, accompanied by water baptism. Trying to develop the character traits of a follower of Jesus Christ in people who have not yet started to follow, who are not inclined to obedience, and who do not have the indwelling presence of the Holy Spirit is a lost cause—it cannot and will not happen. We must not be content with having people "ask Jesus into their hearts." The call to follow Jesus is a call for repentance and faith along with obedience in baptism. Then there is a foundation upon which to work.

Some Questions for Church Members to (Gently) ask Leadership

1. How important is disciple-making for our church?
2. Have we defined what a disciple is, in character?

3. How much does it cost us to make a disciple?
4. How aligned is our programming, staffing and budget with the goal of making disciples?
5. What is our actual strategy to make disciples?

Some Further, Even More Embryonic Thoughts, Especially for Church Leaders

1. Making disciples may not require a centralized "church" building. You already know that. But what I really want to say is that a centralized church building may actually hinder disciple-making. Whatever building you have or use will shape your ministry, and it will be an organizational load that might divert resources from disciple-making. In some cases, a building will make sense, in others it may be better to rent, floating from building to building based on the disciple-making need of the hour.

2. Disciples make disciples. It seems that we are often trying to do with an organization and mass programming what can only be done by individuals interfacing with individuals. Sure, the organization and the programs and ministries can help, must help if we are going to be successful, but it comes down to personal relationships. Disciples make other disciples through relationships, not merely good curricula. "Good community" isn't an add-on to a church, it is essential for us to fulfill our disciple-making mandate.

> "...we were delighted to share with you not only the gospel of God but our lives as well." (1 Thessalonians 2.8)

> "And the things you have heard me say in the presence of many witnesses entrust to reliable people who will also be qualified to teach others." (2 Timothy 2.2)

3. Both the parable of the wineskins and innovation research (I have been strongly influenced in my organizational thinking by Clayton Christenson and his book The Innovator's Dilemma) suggest that the changes required in an existing non-disciple-making church to transform it into a disciple-making church cannot happen. Not that it is difficult or unlikely; it is virtually impossible. New churches are needed if we are going to major on making disciples.

For a parallel example, look at the "success" of established churches in the '80s and '90s that tried to transition from standard, traditional churches into being "seeker driven." This was a worthy goal in my mind, often driven by a heart for the lost, but led to meltdown after meltdown. The churches that made the transition were effectively new plants due to the mass exodus and replacement of the existing church members.

4. The role of music in our churches needs to be re-examined. I have often wondered how there can be renewals of worship (I think there have been three or four in my lifetime) and no corresponding renewals of holiness, evangelism or mission. By labeling our church music as "worship," of which it is but a sub-set, we seem to have made it an end in itself, and poured massive resources into having good music. Worship in the full-orbed sense is an end in itself, but music, alone, is not. While I agree with a young worship leader I spoke to who pointed out that "worship is in itself transformative" I am not aware of any positive relationship between "good worship music," or certain styles of worship music, and effective disciple-making. The level of musical excellence in mid-size to large churches in the evangelical world is very high, while at the same time the level of effective disciple-making seems to be very low.

5. Good preaching, even great preaching (alone) doesn't make disciples. Disciple-making certainly requires information, and motivation, two things which solid biblical preaching provides. But growing as a follower of Jesus also requires relationships with

DNA of a Christ Follower

more mature believers, formal and informal mentoring, interactions with brothers and sisters who encourage, irritate and challenge us, and opportunities to serve those in the Body and those in the World. Many pastors, myself included, have worked hard to become effective preachers and teachers. But all the gifts and all the members of the church are needed to make disciples. "From him the whole body...grows and builds itself up in love, as each part does its work." (Ephesians 4.16)

Conclusion

A Christ Follower is, according to the Bible:

- A Lover of God

- A Lover of People

- Holy

- Truth-based

- Evangelistic

- Persevering

- God-Dependent

- Focused on Eternity

In my two plus decades of pastoral ministry, I have seen some people come to the faith and become Christlike disciple-making followers of Jesus. But far too few. Similarly, it is difficult to find churches that have articulated the purpose of making disciples, clearly defined the traits of a follower of Jesus, and shaped their ministries accordingly. I look forward to the day when a deliberate disciple-making focus and effort in our churches is normal, and offer these thoughts as a contribution to that end.

Made in the USA
Columbia, SC
17 December 2018